Focus in Kindergarten

Teaching with Curriculum Focal Points

Focus in Kindergarten

Teaching with Curriculum Focal Points

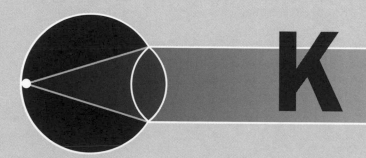

Planning and Writing Team

Karen C. Fuson, *Chair, Northwestern University (Professor Emerita)*

Douglas H. Clements, *University at Buffalo, State University of New York*

Sybilla Beckmann, *University of Georgia*

NATIONAL COUNCIL OF
TEACHERS OF MATHEMATICS

National Association for the
Education of Young Children

Copyright © 2010 by
THE NATIONAL COUNCIL OF TEACHERS OF MATHEMATICS, INC.
1906 Association Drive, Reston, VA 20191-1502
(703) 620-9840; (800) 235-7566; www.nctm.org
All rights reserved

Published simultaneously by the National Council of Teachers of Mathematics and by
the National Association for the Education of Young Children, 1313 L Street, NW,
Suite 500, Washington DC 20005-4101, www.naeyc.org.

Library of Congress Cataloging-in-Publication Data

Fuson, Karen C.
  Focus in kindergarten : teaching with curriculum focal points / planning and writing team, Karen C. Fuson,
Chair, Douglas H. Clements, Sybilla Beckmann.
      p. cm.
  ISBN 978-0-87353-645-5
  1. Mathematics—Study and teaching (Early childhood)—Standards—United States. 2. Early childhood
education—Curricula—Standards—United States. 3. Effective teaching—United States. 4. Curriculum planning—Standards—United States. I. Clements, Douglas H. II. Beckmann, Sybilla. III. Title.
  QA135.6.F8745 2009
  372.7—dc22
                                    2009046148

The National Council of Teachers of Mathematics is a public voice of mathematics education,
supporting teachers to ensure equitable mathematics learning of the highest quality for all students
through vision, leadership, professional development, and research.

Printed in the United States of America

Contents

Contents — Continued

On September 12, 2006, the National Council of Teachers of Mathematics released *Curriculum Focal Points for Prekindergarten through Grade 8 Mathematics: A Quest for Coherence* to encourage discussions at the national, state, and district levels on the importance of designing a coherent elementary mathematics curriculum focusing on the important mathematical ideas at each grade level. The natural question that followed the release of *Curriculum Focal Points* was "How do we translate this view of a focused curriculum into the classroom?"

Focus in Kindergarten, one in a series of grade-level publications, is designed to support teachers, supervisors, and coordinators as they begin the discussion of a more focused curriculum across and within prekindergarten through eighth grade, as presented in *Curriculum Focal Points*. Additionally, teacher educators should find it useful as a vehicle for exploring mathematical ideas and curriculum issues involving the prekindergarten mathematics curriculum with their preservice teachers.

The members of the planning and writing team, all active leaders in mathematics education and professional development, created this grade-level book as a framework for individual or group experiences in which teachers deepen their understanding of the mathematical ideas they will be teaching. This book describes and illustrates learning paths for the mathematical concepts and skills of each kindergarten Focal Point, including powerful representational supports for teaching and learning that can facilitate understanding, stimulate productive discussions about mathematical thinking, and provide a foundation for fluency with the core ideas. We also discuss common student errors and misconceptions, reasons the errors may arise, and teaching methods or visual representations to address the errors. Because learning paths cut across grades, we have included some discussion of related Focal Points at prekindergarten so that we can describe and clarify prerequisite knowledge in prekindergarten and show how the kindergarten understandings build on what went before. Grade 1 is included briefly to see what kindergarten ideas form the bases for Grade 1 understandings.

Whether you are working with your colleagues or individually, we hope you will find the discussions of the learning paths, representations, and lines of reasoning valuable as you plan activities and discussions for your students and as you strive to help your students achieve the depth of understanding of important mathematical concepts necessary for their future success.

—Karen C. Fuson, *Chair*
Douglas H. Clements
Sybilla Beckmann
Kindergarten Planning and Writing Team

As states and local school districts implement more rigorous assessment and accountability systems, teachers often face long lists of mathematics topics or learning expectations to address at each grade level, with many topics repeating from year to year. Lacking clear, consistent priorities and focus, teachers stretch to find the time to present important mathematical topics effectively and in depth.

The National Council of Teachers of Mathematics (NCTM) is responding to this challenge by presenting *Curriculum Focal Points for Prekindergarten through Grade 8 Mathematics: A Quest for Coherence.* Building on *Principles and Standards for School Mathematics* (NCTM 2000), this new publication is offered as a starting point in a dialogue on what is important at particular levels of instruction and as an initial step toward a more coherent, focused curriculum in this country.

The writing team for *Curriculum Focal Points for Prekindergarten through Grade 8 Mathematics* consisted of nine members, with at least one university-level mathematics educator or mathematician and one pre-K–8 classroom practitioner from each of the three grade bands (pre-K–grade 2, grades 3–5, and grades 6–8). The writing team examined curricula from multiple states and countries as well as a wide array of researchers' and experts' writings in creating a set of focal points for pre-K–grade 8 mathematics.

On behalf of the Board of Directors, we thank everyone who helped make this publication possible.

Cathy Seeley
President, 2004–2006
National Council of Teachers of Mathematics

Francis (Skip) Fennell
President, 2006–2008
National Council of Teachers of Mathematics

Members of the Curriculum Focal Points for Grades Pre-K–8 Writing Team

Jane F. Schielack, *Chair*, Texas A&M University, College Station, Texas
Sybilla Beckmann, University of Georgia, Athens, Georgia
Randall I. Charles, San José State University (emeritus), San José, California
Douglas H. Clements, University at Buffalo, State University of New York, Buffalo, New York
Paula B. Duckett, District of Columbia Public Schools (retired), Washington, D.C.
Francis (Skip) Fennell, McDaniel College, Westminster, Maryland
Sharon L. Lewandowski, Bryant Woods Elementary School, Columbia, Maryland
Emma Treviño, Charles A. Dana Center, University of Texas at Austin, Austin, Texas
Rose Mary Zbiek, The Pennsylvania State University, University Park, Pennsylvania

Staff Liaison
Melanie S. Ott, National Council of Teachers of Mathematics, Reston, Virginia

ACKNOWLEDGMENTS

The National Council of Teachers of Mathematics would like to thank Sue Bredekamp, De Ann Huinker, and Henry S. Kepner Jr. for thoughtful and helpful comments on drafts of the manuscript. Special thanks are due to Francis (Skip) Fennell for initiating the project and for his enthusiastic support and encouragement, and to Henry S. Kepner Jr. for continuing to carry the Focal Points torch with equal dedication and support.

The final product reflects the editorial expertise of Ann M. Butterfield, NCTM senior editor, and the design expertise of Randy White, NCTM production manager.

Purpose of This Guide

Special aspects of kindergarten mathematics for all students

In prekindergarten and in kindergarten, goals for children in mathematics are too limited and do not include goals that children can and should learn. On the basis of prior experiences, many children come to prekindergarten (pre-K) and kindergarten (K) with a wide range of mathematical knowledge. Other children—often, but not exclusively, associated with experiences living in poverty and other equity conditions—come with much less mathematical knowledge. This mathematics gap can be closed with effective targeted learning experiences in mathematics before school. A major report by the National Research Council (NRC) Committee on Early Childhood Math (Cross, Woods, and Schweingruber 2009) summarizes the research concerning these issues. The title of the report is *Mathematics Learning in Early Childhood: Paths Toward Excellence and Equity*. This title emphasizes that the report identifies foundational and achievable learning goals for pre-K, K, and grade 1. The report also discusses effective approaches for teaching that can lead to equity.

Curriculum Focal Points for Prekindergarten through Grade 8 Mathematics: A Quest for Coherence (NCTM 2006) was developed to address a major national issue: a lack of clear, consistent priorities and focus of mathematics standards by grade level in the United States. Each state, and often each district within a state, has its own set of mathematics goals. Across states, a particular goal can vary as much as three years (e.g., from grade 3 to grade 5). Also, most states have too many goals. The *Focal Points* are a major step toward establishing coherence and a consistent set of expectations for children in the United States.

The NRC committee used the NCTM *Curriculum Focal Points* as one of the bases of its work on the goals. It recommends that all pre-K and K work concentrate on the three topics reflected in *Curriculum Focal Points*: number and operations, geometry, and measurement. The NRC committee recommended that number and operations be the primary goal. Focused time is needed on geometry as a primary goal, but for less class time. Although measurement ideas at these grades are important, the NRC recommended that only a small amount of time is needed for them. Work on patterns and data can be woven into work on these topics, but not with the same time investment. It is important to note that experiences that address more than one of these topic areas can facilitate learning and deepen understanding. For example, a geometry-focused activity can involve number, and vice versa.

Curriculum Focal Points and the NRC report are major efforts that deserve to be coordinated. The writing team for this book served on the NRC

Early Childhood Math Committee, and two of them also served on the committee that developed the Focal Points. The Focal Points are too brief to provide effective guidance for multiage or whole grade levels. The writing team examined the goals from the NRC Early Childhood Math Report and integrated them into the expanded Focal Points tables used in this book.

Both *Curriculum Focal Points* and the NRC report emphasize coordinated learning paths through which children move within and across grades. Therefore the tables in this book show goals for pre-K on which kindergarten teachers build, and also show goals for grade 1 that will build on the kindergarten teaching and learning. This clarifies for kindergarten teachers and other educators how foundational and necessary it is for them to work deeply on the mathematics goals outlined here. Only when all children have opportunities to learn these goals can they enter grade 1 ready for the goals at that level. As the NRC report concluded, it is vital to close the gap between those children with such opportunities and those without by providing effective teaching and learning experiences before and in kindergarten.

The core mathematical ideas discussed in this book are mathematically central and coherent. They are a necessary foundation for important mathematical ideas that come later. They are consistent with children's ways of thinking, developing, and learning. They are generative of future learning and are engaging and interesting to children. The goals and learning experiences described in this book are appropriate for parents to do in the home, for caregivers in child care settings, or for teachers in schools.

Learning Similarities across Number and Operations, Geometry, and Measurement

Mathematics is powerful because it unifies a wide variety of situations and applies to many different examples. To tap into the power of mathematics, children must *mathematize* the situations they encounter. For example, children mathematize when they notice that there are three squirrels rather than just "some squirrels," when they see that they need to get exactly two more spoons so that everyone will have one, or when they observe that a paper napkin is in the shape of a square but a tissue is not. To mathematize is to focus on the mathematical aspects of a situation and then to formulate that situation in mathematical terms; it is a means for children to deepen, extend, elaborate, and refine their thinking as they explore ideas and lines of reasoning. When children mathematize their experiences, they solve problems; they reason and communicate their reasoning; they represent ideas using objects, drawings, written symbols, or internal visualization; and they connect ideas. When children mathematize, they use mathematics to help make sense of the world, and they also build their knowledge of mathematics itself. They develop and use special "math eyes" that see the mathematics in the world, and they learn the mathematics language that describes those mathematical aspects.

In addition to the general processes of representing, reasoning, communicating, connecting, and problem solving, specific mathematical reasoning processes also exist that are important across all topics in mathematics and that mathematics instruction should help children develop. These processes are—

- *unitizing*—finding or creating a unit, such as joining 10 ones to create a unit of ten, or recognizing that a repeating pattern *ababab...* is created by repeating the unit *ab;*

- *decomposing and composing,* such as putting six triangles together in a special way to make a hexagon, decomposing a square into two triangles, or decomposing seven toy dinosaurs into a group of five and a group of two;

- *relating and ordering,* such as putting a collection of sticks in order by length or determining which collection of bears has more by matching; and

- *looking for patterns and structures and organizing information,* such as noticing that two and three more must be the same amount as three and two more or sorting a collection of shapes according to how many sides the shapes have.

The Need for Focused Mathematics Teaching Time in Kindergarten

Understanding the mathematics content and becoming fluent in using the mathematics process goals require many repeated experiences with the same numbers or same shapes and related similar tasks. Mathematics is a participant sport. Young children must play it frequently to become good at it. They also need modeling of correct performance, discussion about the concepts involved, and feedback about their performance. Both modeling and feedback can come from their peers as well as from adults, and feedback also sometimes comes from the situation. For example, children are often better at seeing counting errors when other children make them than when they make them, and they can respond to an adult's request to "show eight fingers" by looking at peers if they do not know. If they are counting out spoons to take to the table, they will find out they have too many or too few when they lay the spoons at the places where people sit.

All children must have sustained and frequent times in which they themselves engage in important mathematical ideas and talk about what they are doing and why they are doing it. In mathematics learning, effort creates ability.

The NRC report recommends that home, child care, preschool, and school environments need to support children in the process of becoming self-initiating and self-guiding learners. When children have opportunities to move along the learning paths described for each Focal Point, they become interested in consolidating and extending their knowledge. They begin to practice by themselves. They seek out additional information by asking questions and giving themselves new tasks if given the opportunity in their environment.

Targeted learning-path time for specific mathematics goals is crucial. Children need time and support to consolidate thinking at one step and to move along the learning path to the next step. It is not enough to weave mathematics into other activities, although integrating mathematics can be a part of many learning opportunities. Children need enough time to focus on the goals discussed in this book if they are to gain understanding of, and fluency in, them. Even children who learn mathematical ideas at home will benefit from a consistent high-quality program experience in kindergarten. Time must be allocated for more formal parts of mathematics instruction and discussions that occur in whole groups or in small groups and for plenty of follow-up practice. Practice does not mean rote experiences. Practice involves repeated experiences that give children time and opportunity to build their ideas, develop understanding, and increase fluency. Children also need time to elaborate and extend their mathematical thinking by exploring and sharing their own methods.

Research reviewed in the NRC report indicates that children in half-day kindergarten need to have thirty minutes a day on mathematics to learn the major goals in this book. In full-day kindergarten, one hour per day allows children to learn all the goals. The longer amount of time is helpful, especially for children who enter with relatively little knowledge. As will become clear in the next section, appropriate learning experiences in mathematics also support language development and real-life knowledge, so some of this mathematics time is accomplishing language goals.

Effective Teaching-Learning Practices

Children can be powerful and intrinsically motivated mathematics learners if they experience a supportive physical and social environment. Children need adult guidance to help them learn the many culturally important aspects of mathematics, such as language and counting. All children bring to each mathematical topic some initial competencies and knowledge on which to build. The major teaching challenge is to build a physical and social mathematical learning and teaching environment in which all children have explicit experiences and support to learn the goals for each topic area and continue to practice and build on their own knowledge, with guidance from adults, peers, and family members.

Aspects of effective teaching-learning practices are outlined in table 1.1. Most of them have been mentioned in the foregoing. They are summarized to emphasize that the need for focused mathematics teaching time goes well beyond a single approach. It does not mean all teacher showing and telling or an emphasis on worksheets. Parts A and B of table 1.1 emphasize the two ongoing vital roles of teachers:

A. Expect and support children's ability to make meaning and mathematize the real world

B. Create a nurturing and helping math-talk community

Part C reiterates the need for a teacher to lead the class through a research-based learning path based on children's thinking, as outlined in tables 2.1 and 3.1 and discussed in this book. An important part of such learning paths is that they provide repeated meaningful experience with core concepts so that young children can truly learn in depth. Such learning requires focusing more deeply on fewer topics, a crucial aspect of the Focal Point goals presented and discussed here. Just as hearing a story repeatedly is interesting to young children, so too young children are interested in repeatedly reciting the list of number words, repeatedly counting collections of objects, and repeatedly putting shapes together to make new shapes. And just as hearing a story anew

Table 1.1
Effective Teaching-Learning Practices

A. The teacher expects and supports *children's ability to make meaning and mathematize* the real world by—
   - providing *settings that connect* mathematical language and symbols to quantities and to actions in the world,
   - *leading children's attention* across these crucial aspects to help them see patterns and make connections, and
   - *supporting repeated experiences* that give children time and opportunity to build their ideas, develop understanding, and increase fluency.

B. The teacher creates a nurturing and helping *math-talk community*—
   - within which to *elicit thinking* from students, and
   - to help students explain and help each other explain and solve problems.

C. For each big mathematics topic, the teacher leads the class through a *research-based learning path* based on children's thinking. Doing so allows the teacher to differentiate instruction within whole-class, small-group, and center-based activities. This path provides the repeated experiences that young children need.

D. For kindergarten, children need to follow up activities with real three-dimensional objects by working with mathematics drawings and other written two-dimensional representations that *support practice and meaning-making with written mathematical symbols*. Children of all ages also need to see and count groups of things in books, that is, they need to experience and understand three-dimensional things as pictures on a two-dimensional surface. Working with and on two-dimensional surfaces, as well as with three-dimensional objects, supports equity in mathematics literacy because some children have not had experiences with two-dimensional representations in their out-of-school environment.

In kindergarten, children need to coordinate and reflect on complex information in the numerical and geometric domains. Displays on worksheets can facilitate such reflection and enable children to work with, and learn from, complex displays. They can also provide children with practice working and writing on two-dimensional paper surfaces, experiences that some children get at home but others lack and could profit from before grade 1. The use of such conceptual-visual-symbolic pages might be called *meaning-making and discussion* pages to emphasize that their use reflects teaching practices A and B above.

gives children new insights and a deeper understanding of the story, so too repeated counting and repeated examination of shapes help children develop new insights and a deeper understanding of mathematical ideas.

Part D emphasizes the importance of relating children's work with quantities and objects in the real world to pictures of these in books and on other two-dimensional surfaces or pieces of paper. Doing so is especially important for children coming from homes where such experiences are infrequent or nonexistent. In kindergarten, it is also important to help children relate real three-dimensional objects to mathematics drawings of those objects and to written mathematics symbols. At this grade level, all children need to have both kinds of experiences: with actual objects and things and with mathematics drawings and symbols of the things. And both of these kinds of experiences need to reflect the teaching-learning practices parts A, B, and C. At present, too many children have only one kind of experience, which is often linked to children's background. Too many children in kindergarten settings, many from backgrounds of poverty, experience only or primarily worksheets that support rote learning, and too many children from backgrounds of affluence experience only or primarily work with objects not related to mathematics drawings or symbols, reducing the meanings they can make.

Early childhood educators rightfully object to the use of worksheets only to assess what children already know. However, worksheets (activities on paper) can support understanding and increase fluency if they are used after the experiences with objects, relate to those experiences, and are used by adults focusing on teaching-learning practices A and B: meaning making and mathematizing and creating a math-talk community. Worksheets can stimulate discussions of mathematizing in the real world and of visual patterns that are important mathematically. They can also provide practice, reflection, and experience with seeing things and drawing on paper. The real issue is not worksheets versus objects. It is supporting meaning-making, mathematizing, and making connections among mathematical language, symbols, and quantities and shapes. For this reason, appropriate conceptual-visual-symbolic worksheets in kindergarten might be called *meaning-making and discussion* pages.

Table 1.1 outlines effective teaching-learning practices by teachers. These same practices are important for parents when they help their child learn mathematical ideas at home or out in the world. Parents can do all aspects of part A and do supportive math talk as outlined in part B. They can expect and support their child's ability to make meaning and mathematize the real world by talking about mathematical ideas they see in the world and helping their child talk about those ideas by extending their child's language and by helping them to practice seeing and counting small numbers of things. Parents can do part D by discussing mathematical ideas in books with their child (e.g., "How many foxes are on this page?" or "What shapes make this house?"). More examples are given throughout the book.

Organization of This Book

The rest of this book is in three sections. The original brief Focal Points for K appear first, and then the detailed goals table begins each of the two Focal Point sections. The language in the detailed tables sometimes has been modified from the original Focal Point language to be clearer and to reflect the goals and language in the NRC report. The final section overviews mathematizing.

Curriculum Focal Points and Connections for Kindergarten

The set of three curriculum focal points and related connections for mathematics in kindergarten follow. These topics are the recommended content emphases for this grade level. It is essential that these focal points be addressed in contexts that promote problem solving, reasoning, communication, making connections, and designing and analyzing representations.

Kindergarten Curriculum Focal Points	Connections to the Focal Points
Number and Operations: Representing, comparing, and ordering whole numbers and joining and separating sets Children use numbers, including written numerals, to represent quantities and to solve quantitative problems, such as counting objects in a set, creating a set with a given number of objects, comparing and ordering sets or numerals by using both cardinal and ordinal meanings, and modeling simple joining and separating situations with objects. They choose, combine, and apply effective strategies for answering quantitative questions, including quickly recognizing the number in a small set, counting and producing sets of given sizes, counting the number in combined sets, and counting backward.	**Data Analysis:** Children sort objects and use one or more attributes to solve problems. For example, they might sort solids that roll easily from those that do not. Or they might collect data and use counting to answer such questions as, "What is our favorite snack?" They re-sort objects by using new attributes (e.g., after sorting solids according to which ones roll, they might re-sort the solids according to which ones stack easily). **Geometry:** Children integrate their understandings of geometry, measurement, and number. For example, they understand, discuss, and create simple navigational directions (e.g., "Walk forward 10 steps, turn right, and walk forward 5 steps"). **Algebra:** Children identify, duplicate, and extend simple number patterns and sequential and growing patterns (e.g., patterns made with shapes) as preparation for creating rules that describe relationships.
Geometry: Describing shapes and space Children interpret the physical world with geometric ideas (e.g., shape, orientation, spatial relations) and describe it with corresponding vocabulary. They identify, name, and describe a variety of shapes, such as squares, triangles, circles, rectangles, (regular) hexagons, and (isosceles) trapezoids presented in a variety of ways (e.g., with different sizes or orientations), as well as such three-dimensional shapes as spheres, cubes, and cylinders. They use basic shapes and spatial reasoning to model objects in their environment and to construct more complex shapes.	
Measurement: Ordering objects by measurable attributes Children use measurable attributes, such as length or weight, to solve problems by comparing and ordering objects. They compare the lengths of two objects both directly (by comparing them with each other) and indirectly (by comparing both with a third object), and they order several objects according to length.	

Reprinted from *Curriculum Focal Points for Prekindergarten through Grade 8 Mathematics: A Quest for Coherence* (Reston, Va.: NCTM, 2006, p. 12).

Number and Operations

Overview of Number and Operations

The topic of number and operations has three major components: the number core, the relations core, and the operations core.

◆ The *number core* focuses on four components:

- Seeing cardinality (seeing how many there are)
- Knowing the number word list (one, two, three, four, etc.)
- One-to-one counting correspondences when counting
- Written number symbols (1, 2, 3, etc.)

◆ The *relations core* concerns finding the relationship between two groups of objects or two numbers: Is one of these more than, or less than, or equal to the other?

◆ The *operations core* involves adding or subtracting two groups of objects or numbers to make a third.

The Number Core: 2s/3s and 4s/Pre-Ks

The number core for 2s/3s and 4s/pre-Ks is outlined in the table of progression of ideas. It is discussed in detail in the book *Focus in Prekindergarten* (NCTM 2009). A brief summary is included here to foster understanding of what children with adequate learning experiences have been able to learn. Children without such experiences will need extra time and support at school and at home at the beginning of kindergarten to build this knowledge.

The four mathematical aspects of the number core involve culturally specific ways that children learn to perceive, say, describe/discuss, and construct numbers. These processes involve the following:

- Cardinality: Children's knowledge of cardinality (how many are in a set) increases as they learn specific number words for sets of objects they see (e.g., "I want two crackers").

- Number-word list: Children begin to learn the ordered list of number words as a sort of chant separate from any use of that list in counting objects.

- Counting correspondences: When children do begin counting, they must use one-to-one counting correspondences so that each object is

Table 2.1

Progression of Ideas about Number and Operations (and Algebra at Some Grade Levels)

Prekindergarten	Kindergarten	Grade 1
The Number Core	**The Number Core**	**The Number Core**
2s/3s: Learn these four number-core components for very small numbers (1, 2, 3): seeing cardinality (seeing how many there are), knowing the number-word list, one-to-one counting correspondences when counting, and written number symbols. Later coordinate these components to count up to six things and say the number counted as the cardinality. Also extend the core components to larger numbers: sometimes seeing four or five, saying the number-word list to ten, reading numerals 1 through 5. 4s/pre-Ks: Count out *n* things (up to 10), see numbers 6 to 10 with a 5-group (dot arrays, fingers) and extend all four core components to larger numbers: say the number- word list to thirty-nine, count seven to fifteen things in a row, and read numerals 1 to 10 and work on writing some numerals.	Integrate all core components for teen numbers (10 to 19) to see a ten and some ones in teen numbers (e.g., 18 = 10 + 8) and relate 10 ones to 1 ten. Extend the core components: say the tens list 10, 20, …, 100 and count to 100 by ones, count up to twenty-five things in a row with effort, read and write 1 to 19.	See, say, count, draw, and write tens-units and ones-units from 1 to 100, seeing and counting the groups of ten both as decades (ten, twenty, thirty, …) and as tens (1 ten, 2 tens, 3 tens, …).
The Relations (More Than/ Less Than) Core	**The Relations (More Than/ Less Than) Core**	**The Relations (More Than/ Less Than) Core**
2s/3s: Use perceptual, length, and density strategies to find *which is more* for two numbers ≤ 5. 4s/pre-Ks: Use counting and matching strategies to find *which is more* for two numbers≤ 5 and begin also to use *less/fewer*.	Show comparing situations with objects or in a drawing, and match or count to find out *which is more* and *which is less* for two numbers ≤ 10. Use = and ≠ symbols for groups of things, numerals, and pictures of fingers.	Solve additive comparison word problems that ask "How many more (less) is one group than another?" for two numbers ≤ 18 by counting or matching with objects or drawings or by knowing numerical relationships (such word problems describe relations between two numbers more precisely: the difference is now involved). Use the words *more/fewer-less* and > and < to compare numbers to 10 and use the concepts of tens and ones developed in the number core and multiunit objects or math drawings to compare numbers to 100.

Table 2.1

Progression of Ideas about Number and Operations (and Algebra at Some Grade Levels)—Continued

Prekindergarten	Kindergarten	Grade 1
The Operations (Addition/ Subtraction) Core	**The Operations (Addition/ Subtraction) Core**	**The Operations (Addition/ Subtraction) Core**
2s/3s: Solve situation problems and oral number problems with totals ≤ 5: act out with objects change-plus, change-minus, and put-together/take-apart situations. 4s/pre-Ks: Use objects or fingers or pictures to solve the foregoing situation problems, word problems, and oral number problems with totals ≤ 8.	Use objects or fingers or pictures or math drawings to solve change-plus, change-minus, and put-together/take-apart situation problems and also such word, oral number, and written symbolic problems with totals ≤ 10.	Use objects or fingers or math drawings and equations to solve change-plus, change-minus, and put-together/take-apart situation problems with all unknowns and also such word, oral number, and written symbolic problems with addends from 1 to 9. Pose as well as solve such problems. After working with additive comparison situations and word problems (see the relations core above), mix all types of word problems.
Work on decomposing 3, 4, 5 into partners (5 has 4 and 1 and also 3 and 2 hiding inside it).	Learn to decompose 3, 4, 5 into partners; work on decomposing 6 and 7 (e.g., 6 = 5 + 1, 6 = 4 + 2, 6 = 3 + 3, 6 = 2 + 4, 6 = 1 + 5); and see equations with one number on the left and the partners (addends) on the right.	Learn to decompose numbers from 3 to 10 into partners (e.g., 10 = 9 + 1, 10 = 8 + 2, 10 = 7 + 3, 10 = 6 + 4, 10 = 5 + 5) and use these relationships to relate addition and subtraction in problem situations, to add and subtract quickly for totals ≤ 6, and to build the prerequisite knowledge for addition and subtraction strategies. Count on for addition problems with totals ≤ 18 and think of subtraction as finding an unknown addend by counting on fluently and accurately (think of and rewrite 14 − 8 = ? as 8 + ? = 14). Work with derived fact strategies such as make-a-ten and doubles +1 or −1. Give unknown totals or unknown addends (subtraction) quickly for totals ≤ 6 and for +1 and −1 for totals ≤. Use the concepts of tens and ones developed in the number core and use multiunit objects or math drawings to add and subtract tens and ones (e.g., 60 + 3) and tens and tens (e.g., 40 + 20) and to add two-digit numbers and ones (e.g., 58 + 6) and 2 two-digit numbers starting with problems requiring regrouping (e.g., 38 + 26) (do not do such subtraction problems with or without regrouping). Relate mathematics drawings to written number (symbolic) work.

paired with exactly one number word.

- Written number symbols: Children learn written number symbols through having such symbols around them named by their number word (e.g. "That's a two").

The numbers in the number-word list are always larger than the numbers children can work with in the other three aspects of the number core. Children need to have said an accurate number-word list many, many times. They need to be able to say it very easily because they need mental capacity to do other things while they say it, for example, point at objects with one-to-one correspondence or remember a number to which they are counting.

For children, these four aspects are initially separate, and then children make vital connections. *First*, they connect saying the number-word list with one-to-one correspondences to begin counting objects. Initially, counting is just an activity and does not have cardinal meaning, because young children do not understand that the last word is special, that it tells them the total amount (its cardinality). If a child at this level is asked the question "How many are there?" after she or he has counted, she or he may count again (repeatedly) or give a number word different from the last counted word. A crucial *second step* is connecting counting and cardinality so that the count tells how many there are. This step in the learning path coordinates the first three aspects of the number core. The *third step* connects counting and cardinality in the opposite direction: 4s/pre-Ks come to be able to count out a specified number of objects (e.g., six). Doing so requires that counting be so automatic for them that they have mental capacity to remember the word *six* while they are counting. Therefore, children in kindergarten who cannot yet do this will need lots of practice counting groups of objects or pictures and telling how many there are (see The Number Core:Kindergarten). Counting can then become fluent enough that they will have mental space to remember the word to which they are counting.

Children entering kindergarten with sufficient experience will be able to—

- see numbers 6 to 10 with a 5-group (dot arrays, fingers),

- say the number-word list to thirty-nine,

- count seven to fifteen things in a row and count out *n* things (up to ten), and

- read numerals 1 to 10 and have worked on writing some numerals.

They have related all pairs in the triad of quantities, count words, and written number symbols to one another, as shown in figure 2.1. They can see and make 5-groups in fingers and with objects and drawings. Some ways to do so are shown at the top right of figure 2.1 for eight. Five fingers (one hand) and three fingers show eight. The other three visual models also show a group of five and a group of three arranged under or beside the five so that children can see the relationship. The important thing is that the five things be easily perceived as a separate group. Children with experience can also make the triad relationships shown in figure 2.1 for other seen and counted cardinalities for all numbers 1 to 10. The cards shown at the bottom right of figure 2.1 are an easy way to help children practice the triad relationships for numbers 1 to 5 and for the 5-groups for numbers 6 to 10. They can say the count word for either side, and they can match two cards using two sets of cards 5 to 10. Each of these aspects is now summarized.

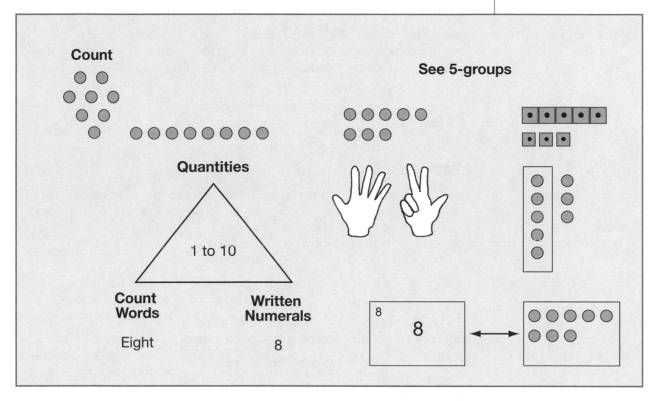

Fig. 2.1. Relating quantities, count words, and written numerals for 1 to 10

Sees cardinality of small groups and of small groups within a group

Sees and says cardinality of small groups

We do not really know the process by which children (and adults) see cardinalities for very small numbers 1, 2, 3. This process does have a name, *subitizing* or *perceptual subitizing*, that the reader may see in articles about early number learning. Birds and primates also can see cardinalities and can say or choose a sign or symbol for them. For humans, the process of such verbal labeling can begin even before age two. This step of naming a cardinality (how many there are) with a number word is the crucial first step in understanding cardinality. It needs to be supported frequently in the home and in care and educational centers.

In home and care or educational settings, it is important that early experiences seeing cardinalities use simple objects or pictures and later extend to more complex objects or pictures. Children who spontaneously focus on seeing cardinality are more skilled at later counting and arithmetic skills. Research has also found that adults can increase children's spontaneous focusing, and doing so leads to better competence in cardinality tasks. Increasing children's spontaneous focusing on seeing cardinalities is an example of helping children *mathematize* their environment, that is, see (develop "math eyes"), seek out, and use the mathematical information in it. Such tendencies can stimulate children's self-initiated practice in numerical skills because they notice those features and are interested in them. Therefore, children will need specific learning opportunities to see cardinalities, but they also need to learn to do so spontaneously in their home and care or educational setting. Asking children to tell how many ___ they see often throughout the day is crucially important. It is important for families to support such seeing of "how many" at home.

Numbers on fingers

Later 2s/3s begin to learn to recognize and to make groups of fingers that show small cardinalities. This often begins when their family shows them how to show their age on their fingers:

- "I am two" (showing two fingers), or

- "I am three" (showing three fingers).

This is an important process because these finger numbers will later on become tools for adding and subtracting. Therefore, it is important for later 2s/3s to work on showing fingers for one, two, three, four, and five without needing to count them out. Of course, initially they will need to raise a finger with each new count word to find out which fingers show a given number.

Cultures vary in how they show numbers on fingers. The three major ways are to—

- start with the thumb and move across the hand to the little finger,

- start with the little finger and move across the hand to the thumb,

- start with the pointing finger, move across to the little finger, and then raise the thumb.

Some cultures raise all the fingers and then lower them as they count (e.g., this is frequently done in Japan). But most cultures start with the hand closed and raise fingers with each count word. Some cultures show numbers one way for age and another for counting when adding, and so on. Teachers should find out how children in their class show numbers on their fingers and support that method. In classrooms where children use different methods, many children become fluent in showing numbers in different ways.

Sees and says cardinality of small groups within a group: partners hiding inside other numbers

Later 2s/3s begin to see and say the small numbers 1, 2, 3 inside other numbers if they have been given opportunities to hear and say such language. One example occurred at home after a child heard similar sentences on *Sesame Street* where pictures were shown with the sentence: The child asked for four olives, and her father gave them to her. She said, "Two and two make four." This process is called *conceptual subitizing* (Clements 1999) because it involves seeing the small numbers rather than counting them. Calling these smaller numbers *partners* helps children relate these two smaller numbers within the total. For example, *one* and *two* are *partners* of *three*. With experience, children move rapidly from the partners to revisualizing them to see the total and can even express this relationship in words, as in the foregoing example. Children need opportunities to see and hear such partner sentences at home and at care or educational centers. Other examples are given in "Activities for Number Partners Hiding inside Other Numbers" on the next page. These issues will be discussed more in the section on operations.

Four-year-olds and prekindergartners extend the numbers for which they can see partners hiding inside. For example, a child might say, "I see one thumb and four fingers make my five fingers." The 5-groups are particularly important and useful both now and later in the learning path (see fig. 2.2). These 5-groups are a good way to understand the numbers 6, 7, 8, 9, 10 as 5 + 1, 5 + 2, 5 + 3, 5 + 4, 5 + 5. The relationship to fingers (five on one hand) provides a kinesthetic component as well as a visual aspect to this knowledge. Without focused experience with 5-groups, children's notions of the numbers 6 through 10 tend to be hazy beyond a general sense that the numbers are getting larger.

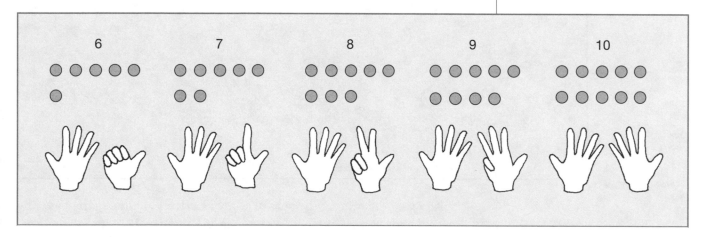

Fig. 2.2. Seeing 5-groups that show 6 as 5 + 1, 7 as 5 + 2, 8 as 5 + 3, 9 as 5 + 4, and 10 as 5 + 5

Activities for Number Partners Hiding inside Other Numbers

1) Adult: "How many balls?"

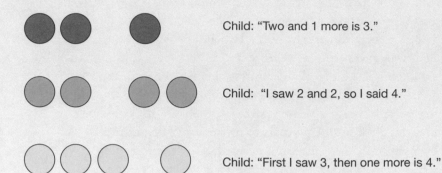

Child: "Two and 1 more is 3."

Child: "I saw 2 and 2, so I said 4."

Child: "First I saw 3, then one more is 4."

2) Have the child make number partner displays (like in 1 above) for an adult or another child.

Matteo:  Becky: "Three and 2 more is 5."

3) Have children look for number partners hiding inside other numbers in pictures in books.

4) For children who are already good at the previous activities, do a "snapshots" version of activity (1). Hide a small number of objects in your hands. Tell children they should take a snapshot picture in their mind when you open your hands. Open your hands briefy to show the objects. Then close your hands and ask how many objects there were in all. Allow more viewing time if needed.

Knowing the 5-groups is helpful at the next level in kindergarten as children add and subtract numbers with totals of 6 through 10. The 5-group patterns are problem-solving tools that can be drawn or used mentally. Children in East Asia learn and use these 5-group patterns throughout their early numerical learning. In grade 1 they use the 5-groups to support their mental methods for adding and subtracting with teen totals by making a ten (this approach is discussed in the operations core). Using 5-groups or other partners of numbers is part of the relations/operations core and is discussed more there.

Children can be helped to see partners hiding inside a number by using simple objects or pictures. The partners can be shown by color, by circling the groups, or as two groups of things close to each other or in a pattern. Objects showing a number can be moved apart to show partners hiding inside that number. With experience and encouragement, children begin spontaneously to see and say partners in the world around them and in pictures in books (e.g., the five people are composed of four children and one grown-up.)

Says number-word list accurately to thirty-nine

Number words to ten

Children begin to learn the ordered list of number words as a sort of chant separate from any use of that list in counting objects or in labeling cardinalities (telling how many there are). Families and teachers say the number-word list, and children repeat as much of it as they can remember. Very early lists may be out of order, but very soon the errors take on a typical form. Children typically say the first part of the list correctly and then may omit some numbers within the next portion of the list. They often at the end of their list say a lot of numbers out of order, frequently repeating them (e.g., "one, two, three, eight, nine, four, five, two, six"). Children need many opportunities to hear a correct number list to include the missing numbers and to extend the list.

Children can learn and practice the number-word list by hearing and by saying it without doing anything else, or it can be heard or said in coordination with an action like jumping or climbing stairs. Saying it alone allows the child to concentrate on the words, and later on the patterns in the words. Saying the words with actions (for example, tapping the head or pointing out or shaking a finger) can add interest and facilitate the one-to-one correspondences in counting objects. Accuracy in saying the number-word list is not enough. The list has to be very fluent so that it can be used for counting objects. Examples of ways to help children become accurate and then fluent are given in the sidebar "Helping Children Learn the Number-Word List."

Number words from eleven to nineteen

The first ten number words are arbitrary in most languages. But then most languages begin to have patterns that make them easier to learn. English has a partial pattern for words from eleven to nineteen, but this pattern is marred by irregularities. These problematic issues are summarized in table 2.2 and listed below. For simplicity we call these numbers *teen* numbers, even though not all number words for these numbers have the *-teen* suffix.

- The partial pattern is to say a word for a number below 10 and add *-teen* to it (the *-teen* means *ten*), as in *sixteen, seventeen, eighteen, nineteen.*

Helping Children Learn the Number-Word List

Parents can say and then listen to the number list in the car, when waiting or walking somewhere, walking up or down stairs, while cooking, and at other times. Teachers and caregivers can lead a group or the whole class of children in saying the number list when they are waiting in line or at the table before snack or walking outdoors.

Individual children can be asked to count in a small group or while others are playing outdoors or at other moments to find out that child's current number list. The teacher can then work briefly with the child on the words that are just beyond their last correct word.

For example, if the child counted "one, two, three, nine, ten, one, three," the teacher might say, "Four comes after three. Listen: One, two, three, *four.* Say it with me: One, two, three, *four.* Now you try it." The teacher helps with *four* as needed and goes on to add *five* after *four* if the child counts to four easily. Some children are helped by a rhythm in the count: "One, two, three [pause], four, five, six."

- However, the first two "teen" words (*eleven, twelve*) do not have the -*teen* ending.

- The third and fifth words have modified the number below ten so that it may not be recognizable: *thirteen* instead of *threeteen* and *fifteen* instead of *fiveteen*.

Table 2.2
Difficulties in Learning English Words for 10 to 19 (Teen Words)

A.	Written numerals show the ones *second*, and teen words say them *first* (if at all). 18, but *eighteen*
B.	Written numerals do not show that the 1 is really 1 ten or 10 ones. It looks like 1, not 10.
C.	The teen words never say *ten*, and only some say *teen*.
D.	"Ten" is not "one ten," "eleven" is not "oneteen," and "twelve" is not "twoteen." We say "thirteen," not "threeteen," and "fifteen," not "fiveteen." Only fourteen, sixteen, seventeen, eighteen, and nineteen have any pattern that can relate easily to some ones and a ten, and this pattern is late in the teens. This is in contrast with East Asian number words that are said as "ten one, ten two, ten three, …, ten nine, two ten" (20).
E.	The English words for 20 to 100 say the ones *second*, opposite to the pattern for the teens.
F	There is auditory confusion between teen and decade words: fourteen and forty, sixteen and sixty, seventeen and seventy, and so on. Most kindergarten errors in writing numbers to 100 involve these issues and reversals.

Children frequently see and use the -teen structure before they learn the exceptions, as in this diary example for a child aged three years two months: "Eight, nine, ten, eleventeen, twelveteen, thirteen." Parents and teachers can discuss these irregularities.

- "What would be better number words than *eleven* and *twelve*? (oneteen and twoteen)

- "What would be clearer to say than *fifteen*?" (fiveteen)

- "Yes, it is harder to have some of the number words we have. But we need to use them or other people will not understand us."

Many children skip over fifteen even when they can say the end of the teens ("sixteen, seventeen, eighteen, nineteen") correctly. This may be because it is in the middle and because it is irregular. So parents and teachers may need to work particularly on the word *fifteen*.

This *ones-before-tens* structure of the teen words is opposite to the *tens-before-ones* structure in the written teen number symbols. We say "four" first in "fourteen" but write 4 second in 14 (1 ten 4 ones). This reversal, and the irregularities listed in the foregoing, make the pattern-finding activity of relating written numerals to teen number words particularly complex for children speaking English. They need help and support to learn to say the teen numbers correctly. These are discussed in the kindergarten number core.

A final difficulty in understanding the meaning of the teens words is that English words do not explicitly say the *ten* that is in the teen number (*teen* does not mean *ten* even to many adults). This anomaly is in contrast with number words in East Asia that are said "ten, ten one, ten two, ten three," and so on for 10, 11, 12, 13, and so on. Therefore, English-speaking children need particular help with visual cardinalities that show the ten inside teen numbers. This is a goal for kindergarten and is discussed more fully in the kindergarten section. It is important for all 4s/pre-Ks to be able to say the number-word list to twenty even if they do not yet understand the ten within each teen number. Advanced 4s/pre-Ks can count out a group of teen objects (for example, sixteen) and then pull apart ten to show the one ten hiding inside sixteen. These ten objects can be in a group or arranged in a column to the left of the 6 ones. Such a column makes the objects look like the numeral 16 because children say that the long column looks like the numeral 1.

Number words from twenty to ninety-nine

The *ones-before-tens* structure for English teen numbers comes from German. The same structure is used in German for all numbers from 11 to 99. But English changes for the words from 20 to 99 to the reverse *tens-before-ones* structure. This tens-before-ones structure is the same order in which numerals are written: "twenty" is said first in "twenty-seven," and 2 is written first in 27 (2 tens 7 ones). So it is easier for children to relate the patterns in the written numerals to English number words from twenty to ninety-nine, a goal for kindergarten. Full understanding of the quantities of tens and ones in these numbers is a goal for grade 1. But 4s/pre-Ks can begin the process of learning the cyclic pattern in the number-word list for twenty, twenty-one, twenty-two, twenty-three, …, twenty-nine and also for thirty to thirty nine. Children can begin to learn this second pattern even while they are working on the teen pattern. A diary entry at the same time as the foregoing "eleventeen, twelveteen, thirteen" example says, "You were standing alone and raising the correct number of ones fingers and concentrating very hard: 'twenty-one, twenty-two, twenty-three, twenty-four, twenty-five.' Each 'twen-' was very long. You count everything. You love to count."

The transition in English words from nine to ten is not clear: *ten* just sounds like another word with no special significance (saying "one zero" would be clearer because we write 10). Therefore, at first children often do not stop at twenty-nine but continue to count "twenty-nine, twenty-ten, twenty-eleven, twenty-twelve, twenty-thirteen." This error can be a mixture of not yet understanding that the pattern ends at nine and difficulty stopping the usual counting at nine so as to shift to another decade.

With practice and support, 4s/pre-Ks can learn to count to thirty-nine, and they are working on the correct order of the decades to one hundred. Saying the number-word list correctly to one hundred is a kindergarten goal, but advanced 4s/pre-Ks may accomplish it. Again, irregularities in English decade number words complicate this task. The words *forty, sixty, seventy, eighty, ninety* have a regular pattern: the ones word followed by *-ty* (which means ten). But most of the early decade words are irregular:

- *Twenty* (two-tens), not *twoty*

- *Thirty* (three-tens), not *threety*

- *Fifty* (five tens), not *fivety*

As with the teen words, the *ten* is not said explicitly but is said as a different suffix, *-ty*. Therefore, as discussed in *Focus in Grade 1* (NCTM, forthcoming), children need to work explicitly with groups of tens and ones to understand these meanings for the number words from twenty to one hundred.

Structured learning experiences decrease the time children need to learn the pattern of decades to one hundred (ten, twenty, thirty, forty, … ninety) and to learn to use this decade list with the *n-ty to n-ty nine* pattern. Without the good start as 4s/pre-Ks in learning teens and the early decades twenty to twenty-nine and thirty to thirty-nine, too many children at present fail to become fluent in the count to one hundred at kindergarten. Even some students enter grade 2 without this fluency. This fluency is important for understanding and then using the tens and ones quantities in grade 1 and grade 2. Four-year-olds and prekindergartners enjoy learning and saying the patterns in twenty to twenty-nine and thirty to thirty-nine, and it is appropriate and important for them to do so.

Counting: one-to-one correspondences: coordinating objects in space and number words said in time

Children must learn to count objects by making one-to-one counting correspondences so that each object is paired with exactly one number word. This task is more complex than it appears to adults, who are expert counters. The counting words are said over *time*, but the objects exist in *space*. The counter must link each word said *in time* to one object *in space*, usually by touching or pointing to each object as each word is said. This counting action requires two kinds of correct matches (one-to-one correspondences):

- The matching in a moment of *time* when the action occurs and a word is said

- The matching in *space* where the counting action points to an object once and only once

Children initially make errors in both of these kinds of correspondences.

- The word and point may not match in time. A child—

  a) may point at an object but not say a word, or

  b) may point at an object and say two or more words.

- The point may not match the objects in space. A child—

  a) may point at the same object more than once, or

  b) may skip an object.

These errors in space are usually more frequent than the errors in time. Skipping objects is especially frequent, especially for larger sets.

Errors in counting

Four factors strongly affect accuracy in counting correspondence:

- Amount of counting experience (more experience leads to fewer errors)

- Size of set (children become accurate on small sets first)

- Arrangement of objects (objects in a row make it easier to keep track of what has been counted and what has not)

- Effort

If children lack counting experience, parents and teachers need to model correct counting of small sets. They can hold the child's hand and help the child feel accurate counting. It is also helpful for adults or older siblings or children in a class to describe how to count, for example:

- Remember that each object needs one point and one number word, and you can't skip any.

- Remember where you started in the circle so you stop just before that.

But children will continue to make counting errors even when they understand the task, because counting is a complex activity. After a parent or teacher is sure that a child understands correct counting, it is not necessary to correct every error. Saying "Try hard" or "Slow down" can help children concentrate and be correct.

Regularity and rhythmicity are important aspects of counting. Activities that increase these aspects can be helpful to children making lots of correspondence errors. Children who are not discouraged about their counting competence generally enjoy counting all sorts of things and will do so if there are objects they can count at home or in a care or educational center. Counting in pairs of children, to check each other to find and correct errors, is often fun for the pairs. Counting within other activities, such as building towers with blocks, should also be encouraged.

Monitoring and Correcting Children's Count Errors

Parents and teachers do not have to monitor or correct children's counting all the time. It is much more important for all children to get frequent counting practice, want to count and feel confident about it, and watch and help one another. Once children basically understand correct counting, they still will continue to make some errors, especially with larger sets. Children who do not show some correspondence between count words, points, and objects do need help until they can do so. Sometimes the adult can do part of the activity, such as the pointing, and can support the child by counting along. Some children need the adult to hold their pointing hand to get the motor feedback about what correct counting is. But for those who basically understand, frequent reminders to the whole class (or by a parent hearing or seeing a count error from afar) about the general process can be helpful:

- Remember not to skip over any.
- Remember to point one time to each thing.
- Try hard! You can do it!

Effort is a big part of correct counting. Children who make the same particular count errors do need support to overcome those errors through modeling by the adult or being helped physically with the pointing and counting. Establishing an exaggerated rhythm can help make correspondences; the child can back down to a more relaxed counting when the correspondences are going well.

Extending counting accuracy

Later 2- and 3-year-olds continue to generalize what they can count and extend their accurate counting to larger sets. Children with little experience with books may have more difficulty counting pictures of objects rather than objects themselves. Therefore, it is important that all children practice counting pictures of objects as well as objects.

Four-year-olds and prekindergartners can considerably extend the set size they are able to count accurately. For objects in a row or objects they can move, most can count with only occasional errors even with large sets of fifteen and above. As before, effort continues to be important. Children who are tired or discouraged may make many more errors than they make after a simple prompt to try hard or count slowly.

On larger sets, 4s/pre-Ks occasionally make point-object errors in which an object is skipped or pointed to more than once. Such errors seem to stem from momentary lack of attention rather than lack of coordination. If children are skipping over many objects, they need to be asked to count carefully and not to skip any. Trying hard or counting slowly can also reduce these errors.

When two counts of the same set disagree, many children of this age think that their second count is correct and so do not count again. Learning the strategy of counting a third time can increase the accuracy of their counts.

Accurate counting depends on three things:

a) Knowing the patterns in the number-word list so that a correct number-word list can be said

b) Correctly assigning one number word to one object (one-to-one correspondence)

c) Keeping track of which objects have already been counted so that they are not counted more than once

Keeping track—differentiating counted from uncounted entities—is most easily done by moving objects into a counted set. Doing so is not possible with things that cannot be moved, such as pictures in a book. Strategies for keeping track of messy, large sets continue to develop for many years, and even adults are not entirely accurate.

Written number symbols

Children learn written number symbols through having such symbols around them named by their number word (e.g., "That's a two"). Parents and teachers vary in how much they do this naming, so children vary also. Unlike much of the number core that has been discussed, learning these word-visual pairs is mostly just rote learning. But parts of particular numbers, or an overall impression (e.g., 1 is just a stick), can be elicited and discussed. Learning to recognize the numerals is not a difficult task, but it does take time and experience. Parents and teachers can support this learning at home or out in the world by asking children to find and say numerals they see.

Four-year-olds and prekindergartners continue to extend the written number symbols they can read and can learn to read the numerals 1, 2, 3, 4, 5, 6, 7, 8, 9, and 10. Children at this level can begin to write some numerals, often beginning with the easier numerals 1, 3, and 7.

The Number Core: Kindergarten

Overview

Kindergarten children can consolidate and extend earlier number core experiences in the four aspects so that they—

- see numbers 6 to 9 with a 5-group (dot arrays, fingers) within teen numbers 16 to 19;

- say the number-word list to one hundred and say the tens list ten, twenty, thirty, …, ninety, one hundred;

- count up to twenty-five things in a row with effort and count out *n* things up to twenty; and

- read and write numerals 1 to 19.

The major advance in kindergarten is the crucial step described in both NRC reports (Kilpatrick, Swafford, and Findell 2001; Cross, Woods, and Schweingruber 2009): Kindergarten children integrate all the core components of number to see that teen numbers are made up of a ten and some ones. The various complex triad relationships that must be understood are shown in figure 2.3 and discussed subsequently along with examples of ways to help children understand and become fluent in these relationships.

A cardinal-counting advance: seeing and making ten and some ones for a teen number

Our number words and our place-value written notation both have a tens-ones structure. We discussed previously how these systems differ for the teen numbers: the ten is written first but is said second ("14" but "fourteen"). The first conceptual step toward understanding the tens/ones structure in both the written and spoken symbol systems is for children to understand each cardinal teen number as consisting of two groups: one group of ten things and the group of the ones (the extra over ten). So, for example,

- 11 is 1 group of ten and 1 one (11 = 10 + 1),

- 14 is 1 group of ten and 4 ones (14 = 10 + 4), and

- 18 is 1 group of ten and 8 ones (18 = 10 + 8).

This shift from a unitary quantity to a quantity with a ten and some ones is shown at the top of figure 2.3 in the drawings A and B. We focus for the rest of this discussion on the example teen number 18, but children obviously

> ## Correcting Children's Counting Errors
>
> As long as children *understand* that correct counting requires one point and one word for each object and are trying to do that, parents and teachers do not need to correct errors all the time. As with many physical activities, counting will improve with practice and does not need to be perfect each time. It is much more important for all children to get frequent counting practice and watch and help one another, with occasional help and corrections from the teacher. Of course, children struggling to make correspondences can be helped as suggested in the foregoing for younger children.

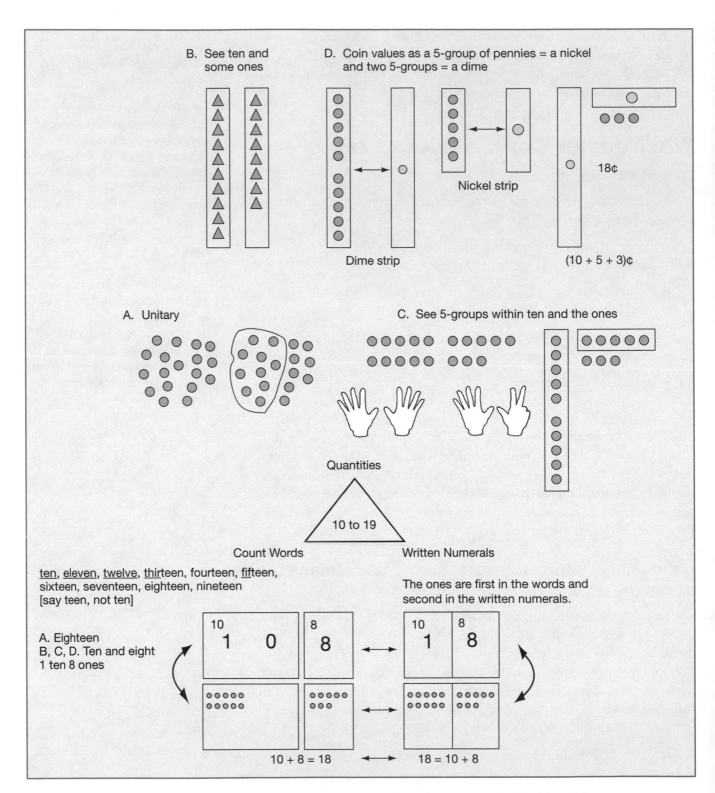

B. See ten and some ones

D. Coin values as a 5-group of pennies = a nickel and two 5-groups = a dime

Dime strip

Nickel strip

18¢

(10 + 5 + 3)¢

A. Unitary

C. See 5-groups within ten and the ones

Quantities

10 to 19

Count Words

Written Numerals

ten, eleven, twelve, thirteen, fourteen, fifteen, sixteen, seventeen, eighteen, nineteen [say teen, not ten]

The ones are first in the words and second in the written numerals.

A. Eighteen
B, C, D. Ten and eight
1 ten 8 ones

10 0
1 0

8
8

10 8
1 8

10 + 8 = 18

18 = 10 + 8

Fig. 2.3. Relating quantities, count words, and written numerals for 10 to 19

need to have similar experiences with all teen numbers. To create this separation of a unitary group (eighteen) to see a ten and some ones, kindergartners need to have experiences seeing eighteen things separated into ten and eight.

They also need to count them and see that the total is not changed by this movement of objects.

Kindergartners also need to understand written teen numbers as a ten and some ones. Cards like those shown at the bottom right of figure 2.3 are helpful in this endeavor. Our place-value system makes these teen numerals look like single digits next to each other: "18" looks like "one eight," not like "ten eight," which it actually is. On the tens card shown in figure 2.3, children can see the written ten as 10, which they know as the numeral for the word *ten*. The tens card is twice as wide as the ones card, which shows 8 in this example. The 8 card is placed on top of the 0 in the tens card (10) to show the place-value way of writing eighteen as 18 (1 in the tens place on the left and 8 in the ones place on the right). Maria Montessori used similar numeral cards more than one hundred years ago. Placing the tiny numbers at the top left enables children to see the 10 and the 8 after they have made the 18 and so helps establish these multiple relationships: 18 is 10 and 8. The circles arranged in 5-groups on the back of the cards enable children to see ten and eight at a glance.

The tiny numbers on the top left and 5-groups were added to plain numeral cards by Fuson in her *Math Expressions* program (2009). The cards were called *secret-code cards* because they show the secret code of the numbers. Children using them say that they can see the zero hiding behind the eight even when the 8 is covering the 0. This is a powerful mental image that helps children see and remember that there actually is a ten (10) and an 8 in 18. This is only one example of a visual support that can help children establish the crucial ten-ones relationships in the teen numbers. Many other versions of visual ways exist to help children see and relate the ten-ones values in the English words, written numerals, and quantities.

Children need to relate the unitary 18 to 10 and 8 in quantities, count words, and written numerals. They need to move from the unitary quantities shown figure 2.3 in A to the ten and some ones quantities shown in B and, for 16 to 19, also see the 5-groups within the ten and the ones as shown in C. Using fingers to show teen numbers (as shown in C in figure 2.3) is also important. Children can flash (open all fingers at once) ten to the left in front of them and then open as many fingers as are in the ones number (8 in 18) and shown that to the right of where they showed ten, saying as they make each number, "Ten and eight make eighteen." They can go in both directions with the cards, fingers, and words to establish robust relationships. They can show the equation $10 + 8 = 18$ by finger flashes, saying, "Ten and eight make eighteen" while someone shows the tens and ones cards 10 and 8 to make 18 (8 goes on top of the 0 in 10). If two sets of cards are used, one student can show the numerals on the fronts of the cards, and the other student can show the quantities in 5-groups on the backs of the cards. The other students can show the quantities using finger flashes of a ten and some ones. Working with the 5-groups within teen numbers enables children who did not have extensive experience with them before kindergarten to develop this knowledge.

The opposite unitary to ten-and-ones order is also important to practice. "Eighteen is ten and eight" can be said for equations (18 = 10 + 8), finger flashes, and both sides of the cards as they begin with 18 and then take off the 8 to see 10 and 8 (in numerals and with dot quantities). Students can lead these practice activities using big cards, fingers, and equations. These triad activities can also be done with quantities in other arrangements, such as those shown in B and C in figure 2.3 or with other visual supports for the numerals 18 = 10 and 8.

It is important for children to see equations with a single number on the left. This exposure will help to avoid the common misconceptions in algebra that the = is like an arrow that means *becomes* and one number cannot be alone on the left. This issue is discussed further in the sections on operations, where partners of a number are written in the form 5 = 4 + 1 or 5 = 2 + 3.

A second, more advanced understanding is the use of a new unit: a unit of ten. The use of this new ten-unit requires understanding that ten ones equal one ten. This is the first step in the full place-value knowledge to be developed in grade 1: that the numeral in the tens position tells how many tens there are. So the written teen number symbols 18 mean 1 group of ten (1 ten rather than 10 ones) and 8 ones. The arrangements in B, C, and D in figure 2.3 support this shift from the 10 ones as a group to 1 ten as a higher unit because children say that the column of 10 ones looks like the numeral 1 (1 ten). This idea can be started in kindergarten, but it develops more fully in grade 1 with the extension of place value from the teens to ninety-nine. The idea of a tens place (on the left) in which you write the number of tens and a ones place on the right in which you write the number of ones really requires experience with the varied numbers of tens and of ones in the numbers from 20 to 99.

Understanding monetary values

Many states at present require that kindergarten children understand some aspects of money. Some stated goals are beyond what is achievable even for many children who have had strong earlier mathematical experiences. The mathematical aspects of money that are most appropriate are using the ideas of a 5-group and a 10-group that have been developed in kindergarten. Ten pennies make one dime, and five pennies make one nickel. Learning the values of a dime and a nickel are, of course, particularly complicated because their values are not in the order of the sizes of the coins. In size, a dime is smaller than a penny, but the opposite is true for the value: a penny is less than a dime. Also, there is nothing about the sizes of a penny and a nickel that shows that one nickel equals five pennies. For this reason, it is too difficult to work with these coins alone. Kindergarten children need visual supports that show the values of nickels and dimes in pennies. One such example is shown in figure 2.3 at the top right in D. A nickel strip shows five pennies on one side and one nickel on the other side. A dime strip shows ten pennies on one side and one dime on the other side. Children can use the penny side of these strips to show teen numbers, as on the rightmost drawing in C in figure 2.3: eighteen is ten pennies and five pennies and three pennies. Above this drawing on the right of D can be seen 18 cents using the dime strip and nickel strip. The penny strips shown in C have been flipped over to show one dime, one nickel, and the three loose pennies that make 18 cents.

Counting mixed collections of dimes, nickels, and pennies requires shifting counts from counting by tens when counting dimes to counting by fives when counting nickels to counting by ones when counting pennies. Such shifts are too complex for many children at this level, especially if children are looking at the coins rather than looking at their values as pennies. Also, any work on the names of the coins (penny, nickel, dime), and on their visual features, needs to be related to visually supporting their value as ones, fives, or tens. It is the quantitative values that are mathematically important. Showing 18 cents in pennies using one 10-group, one 5-group, and 3 ones is appropriate for all children in kindergarten. Seeing this value of 18 cents as one dime, one nickel, and three pennies using something like the penny strips that show the quantities is also appropriate. But making 18 cents just with a dime, nickel, and pennies without the intervening visual support of all pennies as in C is too difficult for some children in kindergarten and should wait until grade 1. Some children do have experience with money outside of school, and their knowledge will often be above that of their classmates with no such knowledge. Such children can help others who are building the complex triad relationships for money.

The number-word list

Kindergarten children extend their beginning 4s/pre-Ks knowledge of the decade words (for 20, 30, 40, ..., 100) to the whole decade list in order: ten, twenty, thirty, ..., ninety. Doing so while looking at the number symbols from 1 to 100 grouped in tens can help reinforce the pattern of these words as meaning groups of ten. Flashing ten fingers as they say each decade word can also begin to build the knowledge of these words as meaning 1 ten, 2 tens, 3 tens, ..., 9 tens.

Kindergarten children also can extend the decade pattern *n-ty, n-ty one,* ..., *n-ty nine* they used in counting from twenty to twenty-nine and from thirty to thirty-nine to learn to count by ones from one to one hundred. Again, doing so looking at the written numerals arranged in groups of ten can help them associate the *n-ty, n-ty one, ..., n-ty nine* pattern to the written numerals as, for example, 40, 41, 42, 43, ..., 49. Written numerals arranged in vertical columns of ten allow children to see the repeating tens number more easily (see fig. 2.4) because these tens numbers are visible on the left side of each column (all the 1's are in a column for the teens, all the 2s are in a column for the twenties, etc.). The tens words move along the bottom of such a table and summarize the number of groups of ten so far. It is helpful to have the groups of ten numbers in each column grouped in some obvious way rather than just have the usual hundreds grid in which the groups of ten numbers are not so obvious.

1	11	21	31	41	51	61	71	81	91
2	12	22	32	42	52	62	72	82	92
3	13	23	33	43	53	63	73	83	93
4	14	24	34	44	54	64	74	84	94
5	15	25	35	45	55	65	75	85	95
6	16	26	36	46	56	66	76	86	96
7	17	27	37	47	57	67	77	87	97
8	18	28	38	48	58	68	78	88	98
9	19	29	39	49	59	69	79	89	99
10	20	30	40	50	60	70	80	90	100

Fig. 2.4. Patterns in vertical groups of ten in the numbers to 100

Many kindergarten children will not develop full understanding of the triad relationships among tens and ones quantities, count words, and written numerals. As always, production of the number-word list outruns the other number aspects. But kindergartners can learn the count words to one hundred. Doing so in the presence of groups of tens visually and with finger flashes can help children build a foundation for fuller understanding in grade 1. As always with the number-word list, it needs to be very fluent so that children can say it in connection with other actions or thoughts. So children need experience counting by tens and by ones to one hundred even after they can do so accurately alone.

Written number symbols

Four-year-olds and prekindergartners can enter kindergarten able to read written number symbols from 1 to 10, although many will not be able to read all of them. Learning to write number symbols (numerals) is a much more difficult task. Writing numerals requires children to have an accurate mental image of the symbol, which entails left-right orientation and a motor plan to translate the mental image into the correct sequence of motor actions to form a numeral (e.g., see details in Baroody and Coslick [1998]). Obviously, some numerals are much easier than others. The loops in 6 and 9, the curve and straight line in the 2, and the crossovers in the 8 are difficult but can be mastered by kindergarten children with effort. The easier numerals 1, 3, 4, 5, and 7 can often be mastered earlier. At kindergarten, learning to write correct and readable numerals is a crucial step. But it is not enough. Children must become fluent at writing numerals so that they can do so as part of another task. It is common for children in kindergarten and even later to reverse some numerals (such as 3) because the left-right orientation is difficult for them. This orientation will become easier with age and experience.

Learning to read teen written number symbols and relate them to quantities was discussed previously. Kindergarten children can learn to write all the numbers to 19. Writing teen numbers provides practice with the numbers 1 to 9 because the teen numbers are just the easy numeral 1 and a ones number 1 to 9. Because of the reversals in the order of the tens and ones in the teens words and the written numerals, children may reverse the numerals systematically at first or occasionally, writing "41" for fourteen. Discussion, practice, and seeing numeral cards and quantities with the 1 (ten) on the left can help children overcome this error.

Written work for triads to ten and for teens

Written work, including activity sheets, is appropriate in kindergarten if it follows up on activities with objects or presents supportive visualizations. Children need practice that builds fluency after related experiences with objects to build mathematical understanding, and they need experience relating symbols for quantities to actual or drawn quantities. This is especially important for the teen written numerals and quantities. Children need to follow up the experiences summarized in figure 2.3 and discussed in the foregoing by seeing and drawing quantities and writing numbers in equations on activity sheets that connect quantities as a ten and some ones and teen equations such as $18 = 10 + 8$.

Pictures, scenes, books about number, and activity sheets need to present quantities clearly. Textbooks or worksheets often present sets that are very messy and hard to see. Layouts often discourage subitizing and frequently depict collections of objects that are difficult to count. Such complicating factors include embedded or overlapping pictures, complex noncompact things or pictures (e.g., detailed animals of different sizes rather than circles or squares), lack of symmetry, and irregular arrangements (Clements and Sarama 2007). Kindergarten children are still building mental images for numerical quantities. Seeing groupings is important, and groups of five and of ten are especially important at this age.

The Number Core: Grades 1 and 2

Kindergarten children learn the number-word list to one hundred. They build strong understandings of teen numbers as a unitary quantity that contains ten and some ones. They see and relate the ten and some ones within quantities, numerals, equations, and count words. They begin to form some understandings of the number words and numerals from 20 to 99 as tens and ones. All of this vital work forms a crucial basis for the extension in grade 1 to full place-value understanding of numbers to 100 and the use of such understanding in adding and (some) subtracting. These understandings in grade 1 form the basis of the extension in grade 2 to place-value understanding of three-digit numbers and the use of place value in adding and subtracting two-digit and three-digit numbers. At grades 1 and 2, the triad understandings formed in kindergarten among quantities shown with objects (including fingers), count words, and numerals are developed and extended by triad understandings that grade 1 and grade 2 children form among quantities shown with math drawings, count words using place-value language, numerals, and equations showing expanded place-value notation (e.g., 58 = 50 + 8).

The Relations (More Than/Less Than) Core

Overview for 2s/3s and 4s/pre-Ks

The relations core goals require children to learn to perceive, say, discuss, and create the relations *more than, less than,* and *equal to* on two sets. Initially 2s/3s use general perceptual, length, or density strategies to decide whether one set is more than, less than, or equal to another set. Gradually these are replaced by more accurate strategies. To decide which is more, 4s/pre-Ks can match the entities in the sets to find out which has leftover entities or they can count both sets and use understandings of more-than/less-than order relations on numbers. They master such situations when both sets are ≤ 5. Eventually in grade 1, children begin to see the third set potentially present in relational situations, that is, the *difference* between the smaller and the larger set. In this way, relational situations become the third kind of addition/subtraction situation, additive comparison, discussed in the operations core for grades 1 and 2.

Relations on two numbers ≤ 5: more than, equal to, less than for 2s/3s

Two- and three-year-olds begin to learn the language involved in relations. *More* is a word learned by many children before they are two. Initially it is an action directive that means "Give me more of this." But gradually children become able to see cardinalities (use perceptual subitizing) and use length or density strategies to judge which of two sets has more things, for example, "She has more than I have because her row of blocks goes out here." Such comparisons may not be correct at this age level if the sets are larger than three because children focus on length or on density and cannot yet coordinate these dimensions or effectively use the strategies of matching or counting.

Children also hear and therefore say the word *more* much more often than they hear or say *less*. Some children initially think that *less* means *more* because they think of the relationship in only one direction (they usually want more of something, so this focus makes sense). Thus it is important for children to hear both words even though they might not start using *less* until they are at the 4s/pre-Ks level.

English has the difficult distinction between the use of *fewer* for objects that one counts and *less* for continuous quantities and numerals. This distinction is not important in prekindergarten, kindergarten, and primary school. Using and coming to understand the words *more* and *less* is sufficient throughout primary school.

Two- and three-year-olds can begin to use the words *more* and *less* with specific very small numbers of things. For example:

- One is less than two.

- Three is more than two.

Relations on two numbers ≤ 5: more than, equal to, less than for 4s/pre-Ks

Four-year-olds/prekindergartners continue to use the perceptual strategies they used earlier (general perceptual, length, density). But they can also begin to use matching and counting to find which is less and which is more. However, they can also be easily misled by perceptual cues. For example, the classic task used by Piaget (1941/1965) involved two rows of aligned objects. Then the objects in one row were moved apart so one row was longer (or occasionally, moved together so one row was shorter). The top row of figure 2.5 shows the rows after one has been made longer. Many children aged four and five would say that the longer row has more. These children focused either on length or on density but could not notice and coordinate both. However, when asked to count in such situations, many four-year-olds can count both rows accurately, remember both count words, and decide that the two rows have the same number. Thus, many 4s/pre-Ks may need encouragement to count in more-than/less-than/equal-to situations and especially when the perceptual information is misleading. But they can learn to use their counting information correctly, as shown in figure 2.5.

When children are using perceptual strategies and also beginning to count to find which set has more or less, they may say such sentences as "This *seven* has more than this *seven*." Such children are confusing two meanings of *more*—

- looks like more, and

- really has more.

They need help differentiating these two different meanings (see fig. 2.5). The teacher or more advanced children can model this difference in meanings by asking,

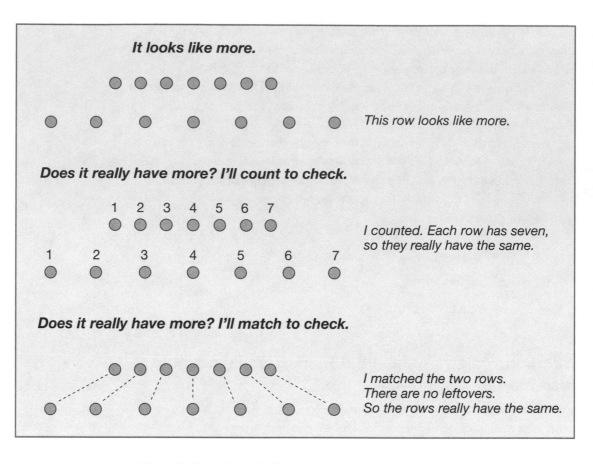

Fig. 2.5. Does it look like more or really have more?

- "Which looks like it has more?" and
- "Does it really have more?"

They might also share their own thoughts by "thinking aloud":

> "This seven looks like more to me because there are things that stick out here, but they must have the same amount because I counted them and they both have seven."

Counting again to check your counting can also be modeled:

> "Oh, I wonder if I counted wrong. I'm going to count very carefully this time and count them both again. I might even need to count a third time to check myself."

A parent or teacher might also suggest matching as another way to check whether the rows have the same quantity and show how this is done if no one can do it correctly. Such matching is often easiest in drawings where the matching lines are actually drawn. See examples of matching by moving objects and by drawing lines in the "Comparing Activity" on the next page.

Comparing Activity

Adult asks, "Are there enough bones for each dog to get one?"

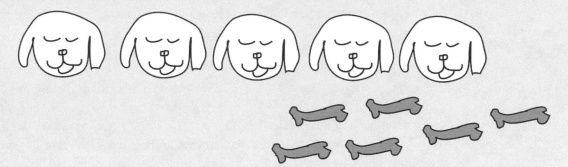

(a) With objects that can be moved:

(b) With a drawing where the child can draw matching lines:

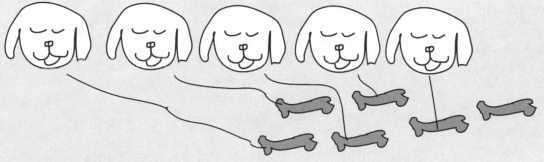

Possible **math talk** for either case:
Adult: "Are there more dogs or more bones?"
Katie: "More bones!"
Adult: "That's right, there are more bones. There are fewer dogs. How many more bones than dogs are there?"
Katie: "One more bone."

To use counting to decide whether a quantity is more or less, children need to be able to count both sets accurately and remember the first count result while counting the second set. Herein is another example of the need for fluency in counting. Without such fluency, some children forget their first count result by the time they have counted the second set. These children need more counting practice. Children also need to know order relations on cardinal numbers. They need to learn the general pattern that most children do derive from the order of the counting words: the number that tells *more* is farther along (said later) in the number-word list than is the number that tells *less*. Discussions in which children make sets for both numbers, match them in rows and count them, and discuss the results can help them establish this general pattern.

To use matching successfully to find *more than/less than,* children may need to learn how to match by making line segments with their finger or their eyes to connect pairs. They can draw such matching lines if the compared sets are drawn on paper. Then they need to know that the number with any extra objects is more than the other set. It is also helpful to match using actual objects, moving the objects so that they are aligned. Here it is also important to keep the two compared groups visually separate.

Before research on counting and matching was done, some researchers and early childhood educators suggested that teachers should not do any number activities, such as adding and subtracting, until after children could do the Piagetian conservation of number task, that is, could know and say that rows in the Piagetian task at the top of figure 2.5 were equal even in the face of such misleading perceptual transformations as making one row longer. However, now we know that four- and five-year-olds go through a crucial stage in which using counting and matching are important to learn and can lead to correct relational judgments (see research summarized in Clements and Sarama [2007, 2008]; Fuson [1992a, 1992b]). It is important and developmentally appropriate for children of this age to have experiences counting and matching to find *more, less,* or *equal.*

For progress in relations, it is important that 4s/pre-Ks hear, and try to use, the less common comparative terms *less, shorter, smaller* instead of only hearing or using *more, taller, bigger.* Teachers can also use the comparative terms (for example, *bigger* and *smaller* rather than just *big* and *small*) so that children gain experience with these forms, although not all children may become fluent in their use at this level.

Relations: more than, equal to, less than for Ks

As with the number core, some kindergartners may not have not had opportunities to learn the meanings of the words *more* and *less* or to count or match to find which of two quantities is more (less). Such children need these kinds of experiences with objects for numbers ≤ 5 initially.

Kindergarten children make three kinds of advances. They—

- extend their use of matching and counting to sets ≤ 10,

- count or match pictures or drawings instead of objects,

- find out and say both relations using full sentences, such as "Eight circles are more than six circles. Six circles are less than eight circles."

The Logical Necessity of Piagetian Conservation

It is true that children typically do not understand that the rows are equal out of a logical necessity until age six or seven (sometimes not until age eight). These older children judge the rows to be equal on the basis of mental transformations that they apply to the situation. They do not need to count or match after one row is made shorter or longer by moving objects in it together or apart to see that they are equal. They are certain that simply moving the objects in the set does not change the numerosity. This is what Piaget meant by conservation of number. But children can work effectively with situations involving *more* and *less* years before they have this advanced meaning of conservation of number.

They also begin the use of symbols for relations by using the symbols = and ≠ to relate groups of things, numerals, and pictures (including pictures or drawings of fingers). The symbols < and > are not used until grade 1. At this informal level, building meaning for the = and ≠ symbols is the most important issue. Therefore, children can build meanings and practice discriminating these symbols by putting them between various pairs, such as a number and a picture of fingers raised, fingers and pictures of objects, or a number and pictures of objects. In grade 1 the use of mathematical symbols can begin to be restricted to numerals only.

Kindergarten children also can work within formats that prepare them for use in grade 1 of picture graphs and use in grade 2 of bar graphs. In pairs of rows or columns of ten connected squares, children can draw simple pictures. These rows or columns of pictures can vary only in number (e.g., eight circles compared to six circles). Or they can vary in color, shape, or thing being drawn. Children can choose the things or the numbers. The important task then is to make statements that compare the two rows or two columns using full sentences containing *more* or *less*, for example, "Eight circles are more than six circles. Six circles are less than eight circles." Such sentences will need to be modeled by an adult, and children may need many repetitions to be able to say the full sentence.

Gaining such facility is an important foundation for grade 1 comparisons, which are much more complex linguistically because they tell *how many* more/less as well as *which* is more/less. The English linguistic structure is difficult because it does not separate these two ideas. English says "Mary has two more than Bob." The number that tells the difference (here, two) is just inserted into the *which is more/less* sentence. Many children do not even process this number word. They just hear the simpler sentence "Mary has more than Bob." The grade 1 book discusses this issue more deeply. The important point for kindergartners is that they need to have practice saying the first comparing form that does not specify the difference.

Children at this level can also prepare for the additive comparison problems at grade 1 by beginning to equalize two related sets. For example, for a row of five above a row of seven, they can be asked to add more to the row of five to make it equal to the row of seven and write their addition 5 + 2. This 2 is the difference between 5 and 7; it is the amount extra that seven has, so such exercises help children begin to see this third quantity in the comparison situation.

The Operations (Addition and Subtraction) Core

Overview

In the operations core children learn to see addition and subtraction situations in the real world by focusing on the mathematical aspects of those situations and making a model of the situation: They *mathematize* these situations by focusing on the mathematical aspects of the situation (see the introduction for a discussion of mathematizing). Initially such mathematizing involves focusing on the number of objects rather than on their color, their size, or their use (e.g., "I see two red spoons and one blue spoon") and using those same objects to find the answer by refocusing on the total and seeing or counting it (e.g., "I see three spoons in all").

Types of addition/subtraction situations

Before kindergarten, children solve two types of addition/subtraction situations: change plus/change minus and put together/take apart. Change-plus/change-minus situations have—

- an initial amount (the start),

- then some quantity is added to or taken from that amount (the change),

- creating the final amount (the result).

Put-together/take-apart (sometimes called combine) situations involve—

- two initial quantities that are put together to make a third quantity (put together), or

- one quantity that is taken apart to make two quantities (take apart).

In story problems at this age, the final amount is the focus of the question in the problem (see sidebar "Examples of Word-Problem Types."). In grade 1, the start quantity and the change quantity can be the unknown number, the focus of the question.

Language learning

Addition and subtraction situations, and the word problems that describe such situations, provide many wonderful opportunities for learning language. Word problems are short and fairly predictable texts. Children can vary the words in them while keeping much of the text. Children can say word problems in their own words and help everyone's understanding. English language learners can repeat such texts and vary particular words as they wish. All these learning activities require the support of visual objects or acted-out situations for children to learn the special mathematics vocabulary involved in addition and subtraction. Children should be encouraged to create their own word problems around their own situations both at home and in care or educational settings. These additive and subtractive learning situations provide wonderful opportunities for children to integrate art (drawing pictures), language practice, and pretend play.

Examples of Word-Problem Types

Each of these main types has an addition situation and a related subtraction situation.

Change-plus/change-minus situations:

Addition: change plus: "One bunny was in the garden. Two bunnies hopped into the garden. How many bunnies are in the garden now?"

Subtraction: change minus: "Four frogs were sitting on a log. Three frogs jumped off the log. How many frogs are on the log now?"

Put-together/take-apart situations:

Addition: put together: "Grammy has one red flower and two blue flowers. How many flowers does she have in all?"

Subtraction (unknown addend): take apart: "Mom bought three apples. One apple is red. The other apples are yellow. How many yellow apples are there?"

Partners as embedded numbers

With experience in the foregoing addition/subtraction situations, children begin to learn to see partners (addends) hiding inside a number. Initially they see one such example. For example, children can take apart five to see that it can be made from a three and a two. Later on, they can take apart five things to see *all* its partners: three and two and also four and one. In kindergarten, these decomposed/composed numbers can be symbolized by such equations such as 5 = 3 + 2 and 5 = 4 + 1. Such equations give children experiences with the meaning of the = symbol as "is the same number as" and with algebraic equations with one number on the left. This is helpful in later algebra learning because many algebra students think that equations just produce an answer and that one number must be alone on the right side of the equation.

Early in problem solving, children need to shift from seeing the total to seeing the partners (addends). With experience and fluency, they can simultaneously see the addend within the total or make the switch very rapidly. A young child watched her mother cut her peanut butter sandwich in half and those halves into halves and said, "Two and two make four." We call this situation *embedded numbers:* the two partners (addends) are embedded within the total. Such embedded numbers, along with the number-word sequence skill of starting counting at any number, enable older children to move to the more advanced strategies described next.

Levels in addition/subtraction solution methods

A large body of research evidence describes the worldwide learning path of levels in addition and subtraction methods. Different methods can give the correct answer, and children can learn more by explaining and showing their own solution method. Teachers and parents can support children in such showing and explaining. The focus is less on the answer and much more on how the child thought about the problem. These levels are shown in table 2.3. Children before and in kindergarten are working at level 1. They use count-all strategies to solve addition problems and take-away strategies to solve subtraction problems. The conceptual embedded numbers described in the foregoing allow some kindergarten and all grade 1 children to move to a more advanced level of addition/subtraction solution procedures—level 2, counting on. Even later, children may move to level 3, recomposing methods. These are discussed more fully in *Focus in Grade 1* (NCTM, forthcoming) and *Focus in Grade 2* (NCTM, forthcoming). The work on partners in pre-K and K develops vital prerequisites for these level 2 and level 3 methods. Other prerequisites for advanced methods are discussed in the section on the operations core for kindergartners.

Summary of 2s/3s and 4s/pre-Ks knowledge important for kindergarten

Number core and operations core knowledge developed at earlier ages that will be helpful for kindergarten are—

- being very fluent in counting,

- knowing which fingers show a number,

- knowing partners of numbers ≤ 5, and

- understanding the level 1 addition/subtraction methods for totals ≤ 5.

Visualizing numbers with 5-groups also is helpful in kindergarten adding and subtracting. Children who enter kindergarten without this knowledge will need extra time and effort to build them early in kindergarten. This knowledge is briefly summarized in the following to support such extra learning for those who need it.

Number lines are not appropriate for 2s/3s/, 4s/pre-Ks, kindergarten, or grade 1 children

A great deal of confusion arises about what the term *number line* means. Two NRC reports (Kilpatrick, Swafford, and Findell 2001; Cross, Woods, and Schweingruber 2009) recommend that number lines not be used until grade 2 because they are conceptually too difficult for younger children. In early childhood materials, the term *number line* or *mental number line* often really means a *number path*, such as in the common early childhood games where numbers are put on squares and children move along such a numbered path. Such number paths are count models in which things are counted. Each square is a thing that can be counted, so these are appropriate for children from age 2 through grade 1. A number path and a number line are shown in figure 2.6 along with the meanings that children must understand and relate when using these models. In contrast, a *number line* is a length model, such as a ruler or a bar graph, in which numbers are represented by the length from zero along a line segmented into equal lengths. Children need to count the length units, not the numbers. Young children have difficulties with such a number-line representation because they have difficulty seeing the units— they need to see things, so they focus on the numbers or the segmenting marks instead of on the lengths. Thus they may count the starting point 0 and then be off by one. Or they may focus on the spaces and are confused by the location of the numbers at the end of the spaces.

It is important to show in classrooms for young children a *number list* (a list of numbers in order) or a *number path* (a list of numbers inside identical objects), such as the squares in figure 2.6. Or the numbers can be beside the objects. Groupings that show these numbers can also be shown (e.g., the 5-groups can be above the numbers 6 through 10). Children can play games and count along such number paths or number lists. But number lines should be avoided because they are confusing. Learning to count to ten and understand the written number symbols are facilitated by games such as the number-path game in Ramani and Siegler (2008). In this game, children say

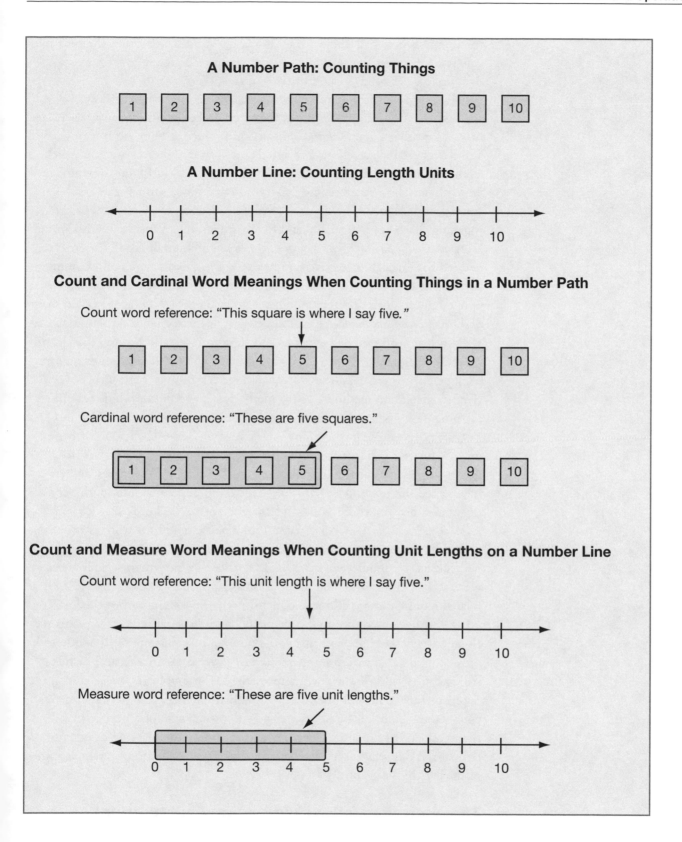

Fig. 2.6. A number path and a number line

the numbers on which they are landing (e.g., "I got 2, so I count the next two squares: Six, seven") instead of the usual counting of the number they rolled or spun (e.g., "I got 2, so I count two squares: One, two").

Table 2.3 of addition/subtraction solution methods showed how children will come to use the number-word list (the number-word sequence) as a *mental tool* for solving addition and subtraction problems. They are able in grades 1 and 2 to use increasingly abbreviated and abstract solution methods, such as the counting-on and the make-a-ten methods. At this point the number words themselves have become unitized mental objects to be added, subtracted, and ordered. The original separate sequence, counting, and cardinal meanings have become related and finally integrated over several years into a *truly numerical mental number-word sequence.* Each number can be seen as embedded within each successive number and as seriated: related to the numbers before and after it by a linear ordering created by the order relation *less than* applied to each pair of numbers. This is what Piaget (1941/1965) called *truly operational cardinal number:* any number within the sequence displays both class inclusion (the embeddedness) and seriation (see also Kamii [1985]). But this fully Piagetian integrated sequence will not be finished for most children until grade 1 or grade 2, when they can do at least some of the level 3 derived-fact solution methods. These methods depend on the whole teaching-learning path discussed in the foregoing and presented in more detail in *Focus in Grade 1* (NCTM, forthcoming) and *Focus in Grade 2* (NCTM, forthcoming). Many researchers have noted how the number-word list turns into a mental representational tool for adding and subtracting. A few researchers have called this a *mental number line.* However, for young children this is a misnomer, because children in kindergarten and grade 1 are using a *mental number-word list* (sequence) as a count model: each number word is taken as a unit to be counted, matched, added, or subtracted.

The use of number lines such as in a ruler or a bar-graph scale is an important part of measurement and is discussed in that section. In grade 2, these related representations all form an appropriate important part of the learning goals. But they are too complex for many children at earlier ages. The distinction between a number path/list and a number line continues into models for presenting data. A *picture graph* is a *number path* in which identical pictures (things) are used to show how many in all. In the simple graphs used in grade 1, one picture stands for one thing. Usually no numbers are present; one just counts the pictures. If numbers are shown on such a graph, they are placed in the middle of each picture, counting and summing the pictures, as in a number path. A *bar graph* uses a *number line* (bar-graph scale) to show the length of the bars in the graph.

The operations core (addition and subtraction) for 2s/3s

Two- and three-year-olds can solve change-plus/change-minus situations and put-together/take-apart situations with small numbers (totals ≤ 5) if the situation is presented with objects or if they are helped to use objects to model

Table 2.3
Levels of Children's Addition and Subtraction Methods

	8 + 6 = 14	14 − 8 = 6
Level 1: Count all	a: 1 2 3 4 5 6 7 8 b: 1 2 3 4 5 ... 6 / 9 10 11 12 13 14 c: 1 2 3 4 5 6 7 8 / 6 7 8	a: 1 2 3 4 5 6 7 8 9 10 11 12 13 14 b: 1 2 3 4 5 6 7 8 / 1 2 3 4 5 6 c: 1 2 3 4 5 6 7 8 / 11 12 13 14 / 3 4 5 6
Level 2: Count on	8 9 10 11 12 13 14 Or use fingers to keep track of the six counted on.	To solve 14 − 8: I count on 8 + ? = 14. 9 10 11 12 13 14 I took away 8. 8 to 14 is 6, so 14 − 8 = 6.
Level 3: Recompose Make a 10 (general): One addend breaks apart to make 10 with the other addend.	10 + 4	14 − 8: I make a 10 for 8 + ? = 14. 8 + 2 + 4 6 8 + 6 = 14
Make a 10 (from 5s within each addend).	6 + 8 = 6 + 6 + 2 = 12 + 2 = 14 10 + 4	
Doubles ± n		

Note: Many children attempt to count down for subtraction, but counting down is difficult and error-prone. Children are much more successful with counting on; it makes subtraction as easy as addition.

these situations. The actions in the situation are acted out with objects. For the adding situations,

- children see the first group and then the second group;
- then they must see all the objects together as the focus of the question, for example, "How many now?" or "How many flowers in all?"

If objects are not present, the child can be helped to count out objects for each of the first two sets and then count all the objects. For the subtracting situations,

- children see or make the initial total,
- then they take away or separate the known addend,
- then they focus on how many are left and see or count them.

Children can have experience in learning how to do such adding and subtracting from family members, in child care centers, and from media such as television and CDs. Children may subitize groups of one and two or count these or somewhat larger numbers. To find the total, they may count or put together the subitized quantity into a pattern that is also just seen and not really counted (e.g., "Two and two make four"). Initially children may need to see the objects that are in the story, but soon they can imagine blocks or other counters to be those things in the story. See the examples in the sidebar "Subitizing: Seeing and Saying Partner Language for Situations."

The operations core (addition and subtraction) for 4s/ pre-Ks

Level 1 solution methods

For totals ≤ 8, 4s/pre-Ks use conceptual subitizing and cardinal counting to solve change-plus/change-minus and put-together/take-apart addition/subtraction situations. They also can solve story problems and oral number word problems (e.g., "How much is one and three?") without objects presenting the numbers initially. This requires children to count out a specified number of objects, which they begin to do at this level (see the foregoing discussion in the number core on counting out n objects).

Four-year-olds/prekindergartners become able to use their fingers to add or subtract for totals ≤ 8. When counting all, they will—

- count out and raise fingers for the first addend,
- count out and raise fingers for the second addend, and
- then count all the raised fingers.

Some children learn at home or in a care center to put the addends on separate hands, while others continue on to the next fingers for the second addend (see sketch "Putting Addends on Separate Hands"). Using separate hands makes it easier to see the addends if both are ≤ 5. Children using the method of putting fingers on separate hands eventually can just raise the fingers for the addends without counting out the fingers. They still need initially to count the total, but later they might just recognize it by sight or by feel. Children continuing to the next fingers for the second addend learn to put up the first addend and recognize the total without counting, but they need to count the second addend. Children who put addends on separate hands may have difficulty with problems with addends over five (e.g., 6 + 2) because one cannot put both such numbers on a separate hand. They could, however, shift to the method of raising fingers from the first addend. Such problems with totals ≤ 8 will only involve adding 1 or 2; such continuations of one and two are relatively easy.

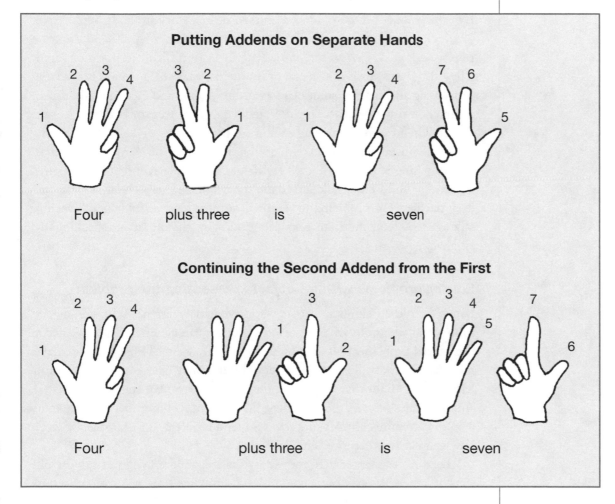

When subtracting on their fingers, children raise fingers to show the total and then bend down or separate the fingers that show the number taken away (the known addend). They then can see or count the remaining fingers to find what is left (the unknown addend).

Some people worry that children who use their fingers will end up using them "as a crutch" and will not advance. But the research-based methods shown in table 2.3 demonstrate that fingers are used in different ways. At level 1 they are used as the objects that present the situation and that are added or taken away. But at level 2, it is the number words themselves that have become the objects that present the situation and that are added or taken away. The fingers count or match the second addend when counting on. For example, for 6 + 3, the child says "six" and puts up a successive finger with each number while counting on from six: first finger with seven, second finger with eight, third finger with nine. These level 2 methods are advanced enough to be used for life. So fingers are a learning tool that are used worldwide. What is important is that children in grade 1 advance on to using fingers in level 2 counting on and not remain at level 1 methods.

Language use

By experiences of relating actions and words in a story situation, children gradually extend their vocabulary of words that mean to add: *in all, put together, total, and, together,* and *altogether* (the most difficult term for children). They also learn words that mean to subtract: *are left, the rest,* and *take away.* Discussing and sharing solutions to word problems and enacting addition/ subtraction situations can provide extended experiences for language learning.

Children can begin posing such word problems as well as solving them. Most will initially need help with asking the questions, the most difficult aspect of posing word problems. As with all language learning, it is very important for children to talk and to use the language themselves. Having children retell a word problem in their own words is a powerful general teaching strategy to extend children's knowledge and give them practice speaking in English.

Solving problems without objects presenting the problem

Four-year-olds/prekindergartners who have had experience with adding and subtracting situations when they were younger can generalize to solve decontextualized problems that are posed numerically, as in "Three and two make how many?" For some small numbers, children may have solved such a problem so many times that they know the answer as a verbal statement: "Two and one make three." If such knowledge is fluent, children may be able to use it to solve a more complex unknown-addend problem, for example, "Two and how many make three?" ("One.")

For numbers larger than they can visualize, children will need to use objects or fingers to carry out a counting-all or taking-away solution procedure. Children will learn new additions and subtractions as they have such experiences. The doubles that involve the same addends (2 is 1 and 1, 4 is 2 and 2, 6 is 3 and 3, 8 is 4 and 4) are particularly easy for children to learn. The visual 5-groups (e.g., 8 is made from 5 and 3) discussed for the number core are also helpful in adding and subtracting.

Research indicates that at present, many 4s/pre-Ks from lower-income backgrounds cannot solve problems given just in number words ("What is two and one?" or "What is three take away one?") even with very small numbers. Such children need opportunities to learn and practice adding and subtracting methods for such problems with objects and with fingers. Experience composing/decomposing numbers to be able to see the partners hiding inside the small numbers 3, 4, 5 is also helpful. Such alternating focusing on the total and then on the partners (addends) will enable children to answer problems given only in number words and relate addition and subtraction as opposite operations.

Drawing the solution actions using circles or other simple shapes instead of pictures of real objects can be helpful for later 4s/pre-Ks. The two addends can be separated just by space, or encircled separately, or separated by a vertical line segment. Some children can also begin to make math drawings to show their solutions. Teacher and child drawings leave a visual record of the full solution that facilitates children's reflecting on the solution and discussing and explaining it. For children, making math drawings is also a creative activity in which the child is somehow showing in space actions that occur over time. Children make these drawings in various interesting ways that can lead to productive discussions. These young children also enjoy drawing more realistic pictures of problem situations. This approach is a good way for them to present problem situations to other children who can then describe the situation in words. Such pictures can help build meanings for everyone. But drawing time-consuming pictures should not be encouraged for problem solving; simplified math drawings are faster and focus more on the mathematically important aspects of the situation.

The operations core (addition and subtraction) for Ks
Overview

Kindergartners continue solving addition and subtraction situations by acting them out, using objects and fingers, and making math drawings. This initial period of mathematizing real-world situations and relating them to mathematical language and solution actions and representations helps children who have not had adequate experiences as 4s/pre-Ks build meanings. The major extension for kindergartners is that addition and subtraction situations are now also represented by written mathematical marks: equations are related to situations, oral language, and children's solution methods. Initially the teacher writes expressions (3 + 2) and corresponding equations (3 + 2 = 5 or 3 + 2 = $\square$). Later, children write expressions and, later still, they write equations. This work with symbols must involve continual relating of real-world situations, mathematical language, expressions and equations, and situation and solution actions and representations. Work with symbols builds up meanings for equations. Then children begin to solve equations presented without a story. They initially tell a story for an equation to continue the meaning-making. Then they solve equations without needing to generate a story for each equation.

The second major extension is that children can use larger numbers. They solve problems with totals up through 10, and they work on partners of numbers through 10. After work using objects to find partners, they also show partners in drawings or on activity sheets. Such partner work is also recorded with written mathematical marks as they complete equations to show partners: 5 = ___ + ___ and so on.

Kindergarten solution methods and representations of story problems

Table 2.4 shows the four types of word problems discussed above for 2s/3s and 4s/pre-Ks. Kindergartners solve these same types, but they now more often can represent the situation and the solution with math drawings rather than only with objects or fingers. The leftmost column shows solution steps for each type of problem. These steps can involve objects or fingers (fingers would be raised or lowered instead of objects put out or taken away). Or the steps can use math drawings.

Table 2.4
Kindergarten Story Problems: Types, Representations, and Solutions

Change plus: Four people were at the table. Then my three cousins came. How many people were at my table?	
1) Count/draw four: o o o o 2) Count/draw three more: o o o o o o o 3) Count all of them: There are seven.	4 + 3 = 7, but this equation means 4 (then + 3) becomes 7.
Put together: There were 4 girls and 3 boys playing at the park. How many children were playing at the park?	
1) Count/draw four: o o o o 2) Count/draw three more: o o o o o o o 3) Count all of them: There are seven.	4 + 3 = 7 but means (4 + 3) is the same as 7. These are literally the same objects; you either think of them as addends or as composing the total.
Partners as separating: Dad made 7 pancakes. I got 4 and my little sister Toni got 3. What are the partners of 7?	
1) Count/draw seven: o o o o o o o 2) Separate into four and three: o o o o | o o o	7 = 4 + 3 These are literally the same objects; you either think of them as the total or as decomposed as the addends. 7 / \ 4 3
Change minus: Mrs. Garcia had 7 lemons at her store. My grandfather bought 4 of them. How many lemons does Mrs. Garcia have left?	
1) Count/draw seven: o o o o o o o 2) Take away four: ø ø ø ø o o o 3) Count the rest: ø ø ø ø o o o	7 − 4 = 3, but this equation means 7 (then − 4) becomes 3.

The bottom-left drawing shows taking away by using a horizontal segment drawn through objects taken away. This looks like a minus sign, so it is a useful connection to the equation for this problem (7 − 4 = 3). Taking away objects from the beginning is helpful preparation for grade 1 counting on for subtracting, where subtractions are related to unknown addends (7 − 4 = ☐ is thought of as 4 + ☐ = 7). Then one can just count on from the initial 4 objects taken away: "I have four, so five, six, seven, so three to make seven." Taking away objects from the end of the total (i.e., the four objects on the right) directs children toward counting down, which is much more difficult and error-prone than counting on is.

The column on the right in table 2.4 shows the equation for each type of problem and also explains how the meaning of the equation varies a bit with the situation. In the change situations, the first number becomes (is changed to) the last number by the middle change step. These situations are represented in the equation forms 4 + 3 = 7 and 7 − 4 = 3. In the put-together/separating situations, the two partners become the total (put-together equation 4 + 3 = 7). But in separating situations, the total becomes the two partners and is shown by the equation 7 = 4 + 3. As discussed previously and later in the section on partners, experiencing this kind of equation with a single number on the left is important for children's later algebraic learning.

The math-mountain drawings (the upside-down V) shown in table 2.4 for the separating problem is a particularly powerful representation for partners. The two legs relate the partners at the bottom to the total at the top. This representation is discussed further in the section on partners.

Teaching progressions in teaching word problems in kindergarten

Table 2.5 summarizes progressions for teaching word problems. These progressions involve helping children build increasingly general, abstract, and coherent relationships among the four components: real-world situations, mathematical language, written mathematical marks, and situation/solution representations. It is vital that the teacher at every level summarize after children solve and explain story problems and help all children relate situations, drawings (or solutions with objects or fingers), and written expressions and equations.

The four steps in table 2.5 above "Mathematizing Real-World Situations" describe how important it is initially to use situations with which children are familiar (e.g., family meals, the grocery store) and to elicit story situations from the children. These can be stimulated by pictures of scenes (e.g., a grocery store with different numbers of fruits and vegetables) or by acted-out scenarios in the classroom. The teacher will need to model the story problem verbal format, especially the question. Many children initially just tell the answer as the end of their story and do not think to ask a question. Asking children to retell a story in their own words increases attention, gives children a chance to speak, and can increase meaning for all children as new words are used and discussed.

The four steps in table 2.5 above "Situation and Solution Representations" summarize steps with solution representations and actions and also with the written mathematical marks. An equation is a complex representation, and children often initially confuse the nonnumerical symbols + and − and =.

Table 2.5
Teaching Progressions in Teaching Word Problems in Kindergarten

Children must link four aspects of addition and subtraction:
Mathematizing real-world situations to understand various meanings of addition/subtraction.
Learn to make situation and solution representations.
Learn mathematical words for addition and subtraction.
Learn written mathematical marks for addition and subtraction.

	Totals of	
4) Children tell story problems for any situation; continue to focus on language.	1–10	4) All of (3), but now solve addition and subtraction equations for totals to 10.
↑		↑
3) Continue approaches below using new settings and pictured scenes.	6–10	3) All of (2), plus children make math drawings and write expressions or equations. Children tell stories for and solve addition and subtraction equations (totals to 5).
↑		↑
2) Elicit story problems from a familiar setting and focus on/relate/extend the language: Children retell in different words and practice the question.	6–10	2) Each child solves with fingers or objects. Some children share solutions and say the addition/subtraction. Teacher makes math drawings and writes equations. Teacher summarizes and relates situations, drawings, and symbols.
↑		↑
1) Mathematize situations from students' lives and from pictures of scenes to describe story problem situations and ask questions.	1–5	1) Teacher and students act out each situation with actual objects. Teacher says the addition or subtraction and writes the equation.

Mathematizing Real-World Situations   **Situation and Solution Representations**

Mathematical Language   **Written Mathematical Marks**

Five has three and two inside.
Four plus three equals seven.
Seven minus four equals three.
Put together, add, and, in all, total, together, altogether, in the beginning, then, at the end, take away, left, the rest

Expressions	Equations
$3 + 2$	$5 = 3 + 2$
$4 + 3$	$4 + 3 = 7$ $4 + 3 = \square$
$7 - 4$	$7 - 4 = 3$ $7 - 4 = \square$

Because the fundamental aspect of an equation is that the sides are equal to each other, it is important for children to learn to conceptually chunk each side. Thus, kindergartners need extensive experience just with such expressions as $3 + 2$ or $7 - 5$ before they try to write these in equations. The teacher can also circle or underline such expressions to indicate that this group of symbols is a chunk that represents a single number: the number on the other side of the equation (this may be on the right or on the left side). The teacher writes equations initially, and only later do children write expressions and then equations. Some children may also benefit from a middle step where they show expressions or equations with numeral cards and cards with +/– and = symbols.

Children can be helped to understand and remember the meanings of the + and – and = signs in various ways. For the + sign, children can discuss how adding means putting together two groups. They can imagine two groups of things in front of them, put out their two arms and grab the things in those two groups, and bring their arms together so that one arm is horizontal and one is vertical to make a + sign. For the – sign, they can imagine a total in front of them and reach out and take some away by grabbling some of them and pulling them horizontally to the right to take them away, thus making a minus sign. For the equals sign, children can discuss how the groups of things on both sides of the equals sign have the same amount, so the = symbol has two little marks that are the same length.

For the simple problems solved in kindergarten, the answer is always alone on one side. So an equation that represents the situation (e.g., 4 + 3 = □) also represents the solution method: You add 4 and 3 to get the answer. The level 2 types of word problems solved in grade 1 have situation equations that may or may not direct the solution (also be a solution equation). A change-plus situation where the change is unknown can be represented as 4 + □ = 7. It might be solved by adding on or counting on from 4 to make 7 or by making 7 and taking away 4. For this reason, it is very important that kindergarten teachers not teach "key word" strategies, where a single word in the problem tells you what operation to do. Of course children must learn the meaning of the mathematical language, but the emphasis should always be on understanding the situation, not just one word. So later on in kindergarten, the teacher should give problems in which key words would lead to the wrong solution so that children learn to listen to the whole problem. *Eat* often means take away the things that are eaten, so children could be asked an addition problem, for example, "Bryan ate three crackers. Karen ate two crackers. How many crackers did they eat?"

In the first two steps of the progression shown on the right in table 2.5, the teacher has been helping children build meanings for equations. This work continues with larger numbers (totals 6 to 10) in the last two steps. But at these last steps, children also move in the opposite direction: given an equation, they tell a story problem for it and they solve it. Later on, they solve without needing to tell a story because they understand the meaning and solution actions for addition and subtraction equations.

Children can discuss general numerical patterns they see in addition and subtraction, such as +1 is just the next counting number or –1 is the number just before. Children can discuss adding and subtracting 0 and the pattern it gives: adding or subtracting 0 does not change the original number, so the result (your answer) is the same as the original number. Because the level 2 counting-down strategies are so much more difficult than are the counting-forward strategies, children do need to be able to give the number just before or just two before a given number to solve $n - 1$ and $n - 2$. But they do not need to become fluent in counting backward from 20, because in grade 1 they can use level 2 counting-on methods for subtraction situations: Think of $9 - 6 = \square$ as $6 + \square = 9$: I start with 6, and 7, 8, 9 is three more.

Partners and addition/subtraction

A teaching progression for partners (addends) hiding inside totals is outlined in figure 2.7. Step 1 summarizes partner work discussed previously for children before kindergarten. For kindergarten children who have had no experience with partners, some activities with very small numbers are helpful. Step 2 summarizes the major initial new aspects for kindergartners: (a) using larger totals (to 10) and (b) looking at and discussing patterns in all the partners for a given number using teacher numerical recording of the partners in addition expressions so that the patterns are available for reflection and discussion. In step 3 kindergartners move forward to written work in which they record partners. They also can move onto making as well as recording the partners by drawing the break-apart lines in any of the layouts shown in figure 2.8.

Introductory work with math mountain representations is shown in figure 2.9. This representation shows the total at the top and the partners (addends) at the bottom. It is introduced with some kind of story that allows the numbers on each side of the mountain to vary (the example given in fig. 2.9 is used in *Math Expressions* [Fuson 2006, 2009]). Children draw various numbers of Tiny Tumblers on each side of the mountain to show the separation of 6 into various partners (5 and 1, 4 and 2, etc.). In the next step, children see one partner and draw and write the other partner. In the final step, children relate the two partners to find the total by adding the partners. Children can continue to use this representation in grades 1 and 2 to support level 2 and level 3 solution methods that relate addition and subtraction and see subtraction as finding an unknown partner (as in the middle row of fig. 2.9).

Many children in kindergarten can informally use the commutative property ($A + B = B + A$), especially when one number is small. Experience with put-together addition situations where the addends do not have different roles provides better support for learning the commutative property than does experience with the change situation because these change addends have such different roles in the action. To the child, it actually feels different to have one and then get eight more than to have eight and get one more. It feels better to gain eight instead of gaining one, even though you end up with the same amount. In contrast, the numerical work on put-together/take-apart partners facilitates understanding that the order in which you add does not matter, because order does not matter so much in this situation. Looking at composed/decomposed triads with the same addends, such as those in the middle of figure 2.7, also enables children to see and understand commutativity in these examples. For example, they can see that $6 = 1 + 5$ and $6 = 5 + 1$ and that the partners/addends are switched in order but still total the same.

Step 1: Small totals ≤5

- See two small numbers (partners) hiding inside a total. Partners may be different colors or objects or grouped spatially. "I see one red and two blue blocks." "Three has one and two hiding inside."
- Tell partner stories for familiar situations. "My family has six people. Three are grown-ups and three are children."
- Children also show partners on their fingers.

Step 2: Record objects with drawings for totals ≤10, especially with totals of 2 to 6 and 10

- With objects that show a given number, separate the objects into two partners using a break-apart stick or by separating spatially. Record the total above and the partners (connected by a + sign) below using number cards and a +/− card. The teacher makes math drawings and writes the numbers (as shown below).
- Do this repeatedly for different partners. The teacher records using math drawings and an expression and later an equation below. Children discuss the patterns they see.

6

O|O O O O O   O O|O O O O   O O O|O O O
1 + 5   2 + 4   3 + 3

O O O O O|O   O O O O|O O   O O O|O O O
5 + 1   4 + 2   3 + 3

Step 3: Drawings for totals ≤10, especially with totals of 2 to 6 and 10

- Children move to using activity sheets that show partners and totals (see fig. 2.8). They move from filling partners into an expression (in step 1) to filling partners into an equation (in step 2) to writing the whole expression (in step 3).

Different visual layouts recorded by the teacher and used on activity sheets help students see and discuss different patterns. The top layout in figure 2.8 shows the break-apart stick moving systematically to the right to make different partners. The bottom left vertical layout allows children to focus on the numerical pattern of the first partner getting smaller and the second partner getting bigger.

Step 4: Unknown-partner games

- A pair of children can practice the partners in a number by laying out objects for a number and showing that number with a number card. While one child looks away, the other child separates the objects into partners and takes the objects for one partner. The first child then looks at the remaining partner and the total card and tells the unknown (missing) partner by visualizing, using fingers, or counting out objects for the total to see how many are gone. Number cards and a +/− card can then be used to label the partners. Or children can make a math drawing, cover one partner, and then write the partner expression or equation.

Fig. 2.7. Progression to show partners and totals

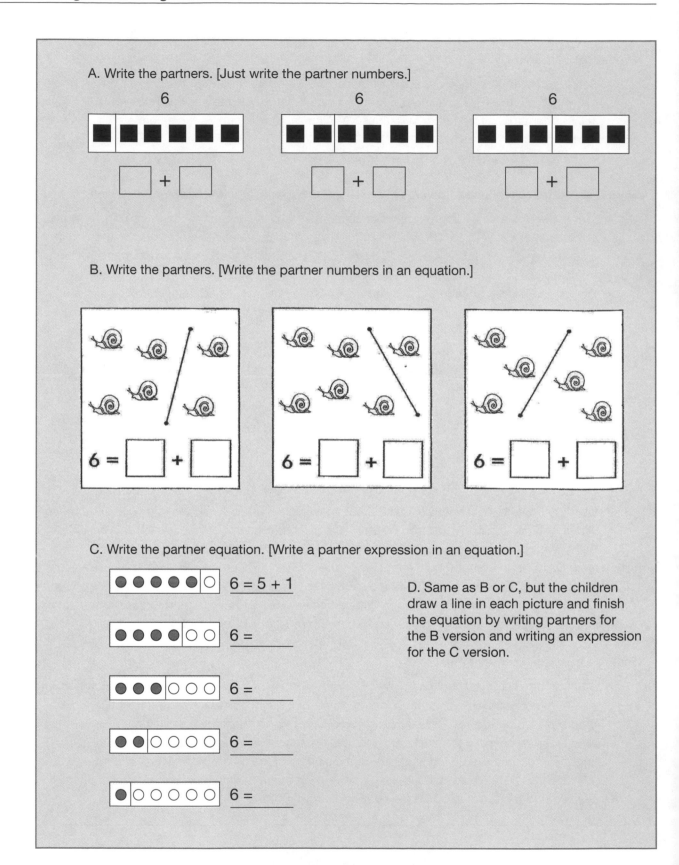

A. Write the partners. [Just write the partner numbers.]

B. Write the partners. [Write the partner numbers in an equation.]

C. Write the partner equation. [Write a partner expression in an equation.]

6 = 5 + 1

6 =

6 =

6 =

6 =

D. Same as B or C, but the children draw a line in each picture and finish the equation by writing partners for the B version and writing an expression for the C version.

Fig. 2.8. Seeing and writing partners

Children hear and discuss a story about Tiny Tumblers who live on Math Mountains. Every day after they have breakfast and do their chores, the Tiny Tumblers go out to play on their mountain. Some tumble down one side of the mountain, and others tumble down the other side of the mountain. They play all morning. Each mountain has a different number of Tiny Tumblers on it. A 6-Math Mountain has 6 Tiny Tumblers on it. Children expand on this basic story to describe what the Tiny Tumblers are playing, and so on. Over weeks, they move through the conceptual progression in drawings of the types below.

A. Draw Tiny Tumblers on the Math Mountains.

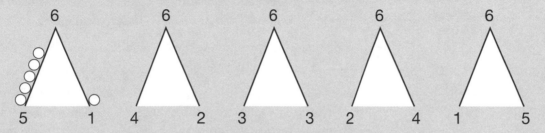

B. Draw Tiny Tumblers on the Math Mountains. Write the partners.

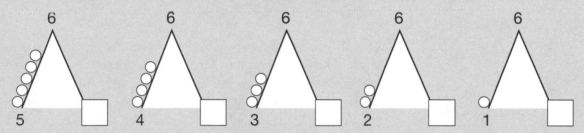

C. Draw Tiny Tumblers and write how many are on each Math Mountain.

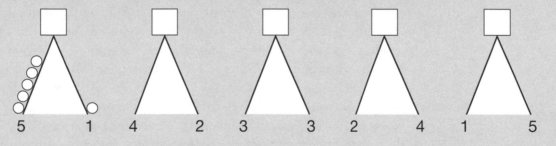

Fig. 2.9. A progression for seeing partners and totals in Math Mountains

Developing the prerequisites for level 2 and level 3 methods

Kindergarten children are learning general level 1 numerical solution methods that they can extend to larger numbers. Simultaneously they are becoming fluent with these processes and with the number-word list so that they can advance in grade 1 to the level 2 counting-on methods that are needed to solve single-digit sums and differences with totals over ten. The work with partners supports level 2 counting-on thinking. Late in the kindergarten year, children can begin to practice another prerequisite for counting on: they can start to count at a given number instead of always at one (thereby connecting a prerequisite number-word-list skill to count and cardinal meanings as discussed in the foregoing).

Kindergarten children are also working on all the prerequisites for the level 3 derived fact methods, such as make-a-ten (see table 2.3).

- One prerequisite, seeing the tens in teen numbers ($10 + 3 = 13$), was discussed in the number core.

- A second prerequisite is knowing all the partners to 10. The first step in the make-a-ten method is breaking the smaller number into the part that will make ten and the rest: $8 + 6 = 8 + 2$ (to make ten) $+ 4$.

- The third prerequisite is knowing all the partners of numbers below ten so that you can complete the last step above: know that 6 breaks apart into 2 and 4.

Children in many East Asian countries develop these prerequisites before first grade. They are consolidated in early first grade and then used in the grade 1 units teaching make-a-ten for addition and for subtraction. A similar approach could be used in the United States if children were supported to develop the prerequisites in kindergarten.

The roles of worksheets in kindergarten

The number, relations, and operations goals require kindergarten children to coordinate language, written mathematics symbols, and quantities shown in objects or drawings (and increasingly, mentally). Although kindergarten children need to act on objects initially, this becomes increasingly messy and complex with larger numbers and more complex ideas. We have seen how the learning progressions for tens in teens, for story problem solving related to equations, and work with partners of a number move from use of objects to use of drawings that children make themselves and of drawings of quantities and symbols with which children interact. It is important for children to have these experiences with conceptual-visual-symbolic worksheets. Because the term *worksheets* so often has rote connotations, especially for younger children, it might be better to call such conceptual-visual-symbolic pages *meaning-making and discussion* pages. This new term is a reminder that work with any such pages needs to reflect the central parts of table 1.1 about effective teaching-learning practices. These pages that connect mathematical language and symbols to quantities and to actions in the world are used by the teacher to lead children's attention across these crucial aspects to help them see patterns and make connections within a nurturing and helping math-talk community. Students explain concepts and help each other when they are practicing and engaging in meaning-making with written mathematical symbols, and they reflect on, and talk about, their mathematical thinking.

3 Geometry, Spatial Reasoning, and Measurement

Geometry, spatial reasoning, and measurement are essential areas in children's development. Children learn about geometric shapes and structures as important topics in themselves. But these topics also support children's learning of other mathematics, such as number, arithmetic, and patterns. Spatial reasoning complements geometric knowledge. Spatial reasoning includes spatial orientation—knowing how to get around in the world—and spatial visualization—knowing how to build and manipulative objects mentally, including composing and decomposing objects. Geometric measurement rounds out the core components. *Geometry* means "earth measure," and geometry, spatial reasoning, and measurement are topics that connect to each other and to other mathematics and that connect mathematics to real-world situations. For example, these core components are the foundations of number lines, arrays in multiplication, fractions, graphing, and topics beyond. They also lie at the heart of physics, chemistry, biology, geology and geography, and art and architecture. So, across many areas, we see that a picture—or diagram or figure—can be "worth a thousand words." Increasing students' sophistication with visualization and imagery increases the meaning they can take from that "picture," including those seen daily on television, in video games, on GPS maps, and so forth.

Unfortunately, geometry and measurement are two of U.S. students' weakest topics in mathematics. Even in kindergarten, children in the U.S. know less about shape than children in other countries. Fortunately, they know enough to build on, they can learn a lot quickly, and they enjoy engaging with shapes, space, and measurements. Indeed, young children *play* with shapes and geometric structures naturally. In a study of the mathematics that children engage in spontaneously in their play, the most frequent topic was shapes and structures.

Geometry

From the earliest years, children learn about shape and use shapes to learn. In learning the *geometry* of shapes, they progress through increasingly powerful levels of thinking about shapes. For example, at first, they cannot explicitly distinguish circles, triangles, and squares from nonexamples. They gradually develop richer visual templates for these categories and eventually learn about the parts and attributes of the shapes. This is especially important if they did not receive high-quality geometric experiences in preschool, because shape research suggests that concepts can become inflexible by the end of kindergarten or first grade.

Table 3.1 presents the developmental progressions for ideas and skills for geometry and spatial reasoning.

Table 3.1
Progression of Ideas and Skills for Geometry, Spatial Reasoning, and Measurement

Prekindergarten	Kindergarten	Grade 1
Shape and Structure	**Shape and Structure**	**Shape and Structure**
2s/3s: Recognize two-dimensional shapes informally (including at least circles, squares, then triangles, rectangles) in different orientations. Discriminate between two-dimensional and three-dimensional shapes intuitively, marked by accurate matching or naming. See and describe pictures of objects (e.g., recognize a three-dimensional object on a two-dimensional page of a book). 4s/pre-Ks: Recognize and describe two-dimensional shapes regardless of orientation, size, and shape (including circles and half-/quarter-circles, squares and rectangles, triangles, and regular rhombi, trapezoids, hexagons). Describe shapes by number of sides and/or corners (up to the number they can count) and sides of same or different length. Describe the difference between two-dimensional and three-dimensional shapes, and name common three-dimensional shapes informally or with mathematical names ("ball"/sphere; "box" or rectangular prism, "rectangular block" or "triangular block"; "can"/cylinder).	Recognize and describe a wide variety of two-dimensional shapes (e.g., octagons, parallelograms, convex/concave figures) regardless of orientation, size, and shape. Sort shapes by number of sides and/or corners and length relationships between sides. Recognize and name common three-dimensional shapes (including real-world objects), including spheres, cylinders, [rectangular] prisms, and pyramids.	Name most common shapes, including rhombuses, without making such mistakes as calling ovals "circles." Recognize (at least) right angles, so distinguishing between a rectangle and a parallelogram without right angles. Use manipulatives representing parts of shapes, such as sides and angle "connectors," to make a shape that is completely correct on the basis of knowledge of components and relationships.
Spatial Relations	**Spatial Relations**	**Spatial Relations**
2s/3s: Enact spatial movements informally using such relational terms as *up, down, on, off,* and *under.* 4s/pre-Ks: Match shapes by intuitively using geometric motions to superimpose them. Use relational words of proximity, such as *beside, next to,* and *between,* referring to a two-dimensional environment. Match the faces of three-dimensional shapes to two-dimensional shapes, naming the two-dimensional shapes.	Begin to use relational language of *right* and *left.* Identify and create symmetric figures (e.g., mirrors as reflections).	Use geometric motions to create symmetric figures (e.g., paper folding; also mirrors as reflections) and determine congruence.
Compositions and Decompositions in Space	**Compositions and Decompositions in Space**	**Compositions and Decompositions in Space**
2s/3s: Solve simple puzzles involving things in the world. Create pictures by representing single objects, each with a different shape. Combine unit blocks by stacking. 4s/pre-Ks: Move shapes using slides and flips, and turn them to combine shapes to build pictures. Copy a design shown on a grid, placing squares and rectangles onto squared-grid paper. Combine building blocks using multiple spatial relations to produce composite shapes (arches, enclosures, corners, and crosses).	Create pattern-block designs (those with multiples of 60-degree and 120-degree angles). Create compositions and complete puzzles with systematicity and anticipation, using a variety of shape sets (e.g., pattern blocks; rectangular grids with squares, right triangles, and rectangles; tangrams). Build simple three-dimensional structures from pictured models.	Make new two-dimensional shapes, shape structures out of smaller shapes, and substitute groups of shapes for other shapes to create new shapes in different ways. (See related area goals.)

Table 3.1—*Continued*

Prekindergarten	Kindergarten	Grade 1
Concept of Measurement	**Concept of Measurement**	**Concept of Measurement**
2s/3s: Identify two-dimensional and three-dimensional objects as "the same" or "different" in size. 4s/pre-Ks: Identify objects and drawings as "more" or "less" on the basis of attributes they can identify (and later can measure), such as length and area, and solve problems by making direct comparisons of objects on the basis of those attributes.	Use measurable attributes, such as length or area, to solve problems by comparing and ordering objects.	Compose and decompose plane and solid shapes, thus building an understanding of part-whole relationships and developing the background for working with units composed of units. (These relate to the geometry goals.)
Length	**Length**	**Length**
2s/3s: Intuitively recognize length as extent of one-dimensional space. Compare two objects directly, noting equality or inequality. 4s/pre-Ks: Begin to measure by laying units end to end. Understand that lengths can be concatenated to make a new length.	Compare the lengths of two objects both directly (by comparing them with each other) and indirectly (by comparing both with a third object), and order several objects according to length (even if differences between consecutive lengths are small). Measure by laying units end to end, covering the whole without gaps, and count the units to find the total length.	Measure by repeated use of a unit, and apply the resulting measures to comparison situations.
Area	**Area**	**Area**
2s/3s: Use side-matching strategies in comparing areas. 4s/pre-Ks: Compare areas for tasks that suggest superposition or show decomposition into squares.	Cover a rectangular region with square units. Count squares in rectangular arrays correctly and (increasingly) systematically.	Make and draw coverings of simple rectangular regions with square units. For rectangles two squares high or wide, count the rows or columns of two by twos.
Volume	**Volume**	**Volume**
2s/3s: Identify capacity or volume as attribute. 4s/pre-Ks: Compare two containers directly by pouring.	Compare two containers using a third container and (at least implicitly) transitive reasoning. Fill rectangular containers with cubes and/or make rectangular prisms ("buildings") from layers of blocks.	Fill rectangular containers with cubes, completing one layer at a time with cubes, and/or make rectangular prisms ("buildings") from layers of blocks.

Note: Some compositions and decompositions activities overlap with measurement (area and volume). Grade 3 develops the area work above as a setting for multiplication. Fuller development of area is a grade 4 Focal Point, and fuller development of volume is a grade 5 Focal Point.

Shape and Structure

Kindergartners form visual templates, or models of shape categories. For example, children recognize a shape as a rectangle because "it looks like a door." Because children base their understanding of shapes on examples, they need to experience a rich variety of shapes in each shape category so that their mental models are not overly restricted. For example, children without good experiences often reject both triangles and rectangles that are "too skinny" or "not wide enough."

Children should see examples of rectangles that are long and skinny, and they should contrast rectangles with nonrectangles that appear similar but do not have an important defining attribute (see fig. 3.1). Similarly, they should see examples of triangles that have sides of three different lengths, and they should contrast triangles with nontriangles (see fig. 3.2).

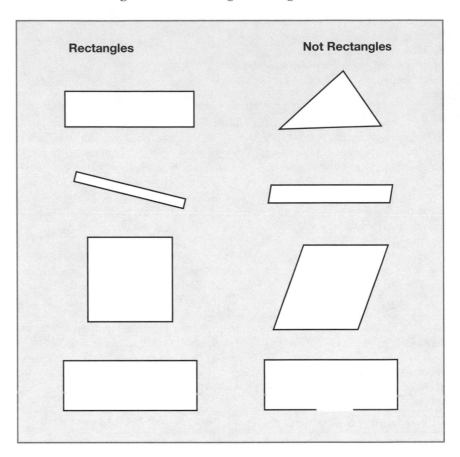

Fig. 3.1. Rectangles and nonrectangles

Children also need to see examples of shapes beyond circles, squares, rectangles, and triangles. Without these, children develop limited notions. For example, many children come to believe incorrectly that a geometric figure such as a trapezoid "is not a shape" because it is not a shape for which they know a name (and many know only "circle," "square," "triangle," and "rectangle"). Kindergartners can learn to recognize not only trapezoids but such shapes as rhombuses, parallelograms, and octagons. Figure 3.3 provides information for the teacher about several two-dimensional geometric shapes. The term "two-dimensional shapes" means flat shapes (e.g., plane shapes that could be drawn in their entirety on paper) that are *closed*, meaning that they have no "loose, dangling ends," and are *connected*, meaning that they are in one single piece and do not have sides that cross each other.

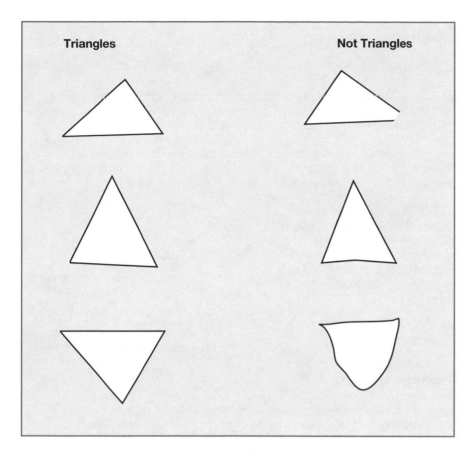

Fig. 3.2. Triangles and nontriangles

Kindergartners should also learn to recognize these shapes whether they are in "standard position" or rotated so that their bases are not horizontal. Although it is especially important to provide varied examples for children who have not had a good preschool experience, development of flexible, accurate "visual thinking" should continue throughout children's education, even as more mathematically explicit and sophisticated levels of thinking and language take precedence.

Kindergartners can begin to develop such explicit and sophisticated levels of thinking and communication. They can learn to describe, and even define, shapes in terms of their *parts* or *attributes* (properties). For example, they can build accurate representations of shapes from physical models of line segments, such as sticks. As they discuss what they have built, attributes of the shapes will arise naturally. That is, they may say that what they build is a rectangle *because* it has two pairs of sides that are equal in length and all right angles. This experience of discussing attributes of rectangles helps children begin to understand the *geometric structure* of all rectangles at an explicit level of thinking.

Similarly, when guided by the teacher, children notice symmetry not only in shapes, such as rectangles, but in their environment. They begin to design and extend symmetry into their block buildings and artwork.

Definitions of Familiar Two-Dimensional Shapes

Triangles are those two-dimensional shapes that have three straight sides (see fig. 3.2).

Rectangles are those two-dimensional shapes that have four straight sides and four right angles (see fig. 3.1). Corners of standard pieces of paper are usually (approximately) right angles. You can make right angles using doublefolding (see the sidebar box "What Are Right Angles?").

Squares are those two-dimensional shapes that have four straight sides of the same length and have four right angles. Notice that any square is also a rectangle because it has four straight sides and four right angles. So squares could be defined as special rectangles that have all sides the same length.

Informally, circles are those two-dimensional shapes that are "perfectly round." From a mathematical perspective, however, circle are those two-dimensional shapes that consist of all points that are a fixed distance from a fixed center point. Any simple tool (such as a compass or even a pencil tied to a fixed length of string) that holds a pencil point a fixed distance away from a center point will draw a circle, as shown here.

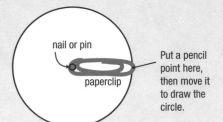

A circle consists of all the locations that are a fixed distance (here: a paperclip length) away from a fixed point (here: the nail).

Definitions of Other Two-Dimensional Shapes

Quadrilaterals are those two-dimensional shapes that have four straight sides. Notice that squares and rectangles (as well as rhombuses, parallelograms, and trapezoids) are also quadrilaterals because these shapes have four straight sides.

Rhombuses are those two-dimensional shapes that have four straight sides of the same length. Notice that every square is also a rhombus because it has four sides of the same length.

Parallelograms are those two-dimensional shapes that have four straight sides and for which each pair of opposite sides are parallel. Informally, two straight sides are parallel if it is possible to slide one without turning so that both lie on the same straight line. Or two are parallel if when both are extended to become infinitely long straight lines, they never meet.

Trapezoids are those two-dimensional shapes that have four straight sides and at least one pair of parallel sides. (Some people define trapezoids as those two-dimensional shapes that have four straight sides and exactly one pair of parallel sides.)

Pentagons are those two-dimensional shapes that have five straight sides.

Hexagons are those two-dimensional shapes that have six straight sides.

Octagons are those two-dimensional shapes that have eight straight sides.

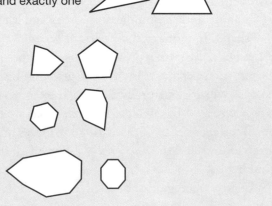

Fig. 3.3. Familiar two-dimensional shapes

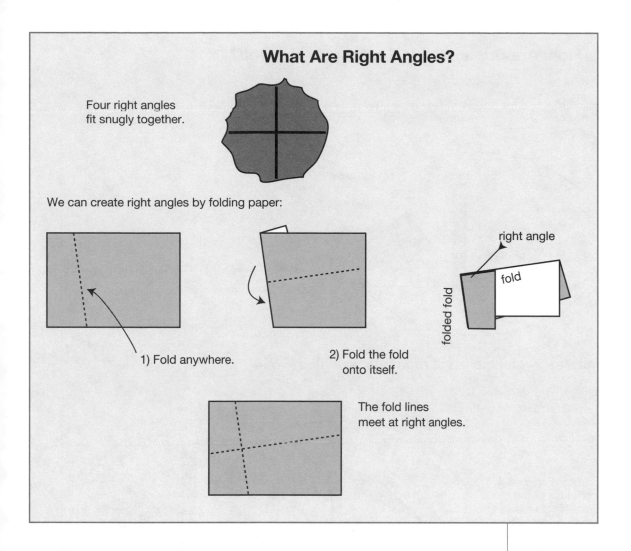

What Are Right Angles?

Four right angles fit snugly together.

We can create right angles by folding paper:

1) Fold anywhere.

2) Fold the fold onto itself.

folded fold

right angle

fold

The fold lines meet at right angles.

Another valuable activity is the tactile-kinesthetic exploration of shapes—feeling shapes hidden in a box. Even if previously done in preschool, this activity can grow with children. Kindergartners can name the shape they are feeling rather than just match shapes. After this, they can extend the activity further as they *describe* the shape without using its name, so that their friends can name the shape. In this way, children learn the properties of the shape, moving from intuitive to explicit, verbalized knowledge. All these variations can be repeated with less familiar shapes.

Such activities help children learn to identify and describe shapes by the number of their sides or corners, as illustrated by a kindergartner who declared that an obtuse ("long and skinny") triangle "*must* be a triangle because it has three sides." Such descriptions build geometric concepts but also reasoning skills and language. They encourage children to view shapes analytically. Children begin to describe some shapes in terms of their properties, such as saying that squares have four sides of *equal length*. They informally describe properties of blocks in functional contexts, such as that some blocks roll and others do not.

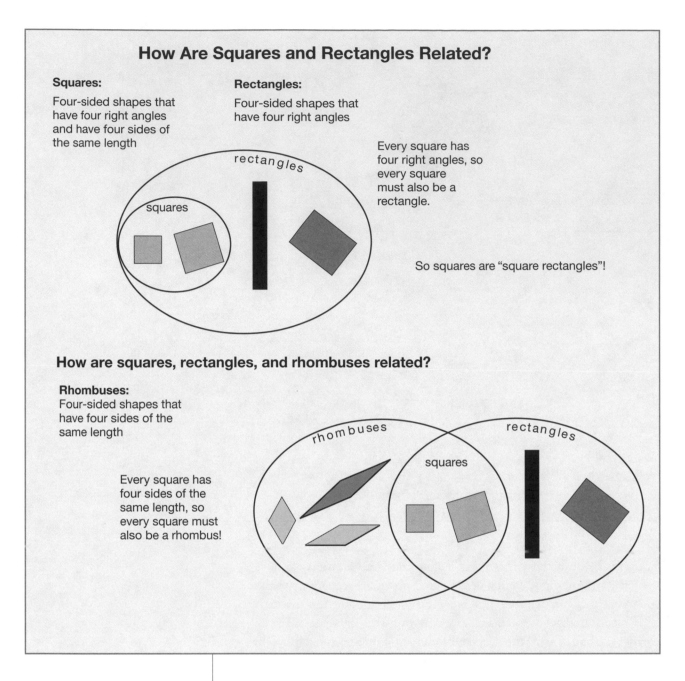

How Are Squares and Rectangles Related?

Squares:

Four-sided shapes that have four right angles and have four sides of the same length

Rectangles:

Four-sided shapes that have four right angles

Every square has four right angles, so every square must also be a rectangle.

So squares are "square rectangles"!

rectangles

squares

How are squares, rectangles, and rhombuses related?

Rhombuses:
Four-sided shapes that have four sides of the same length

Every square has four sides of the same length, so every square must also be a rhombus!

rhombuses

squares

rectangles

Computer-based activities can also contribute to children's thinking about shapes, their components, and their relationships to other shapes. Their advantages include greater control and flexibility, as well as linking the visual to the symbolic and abstract (see the sidebar box on using a computer program to make rectangles).

Unfortunately, most U.S. children are not introduced to such strong conceptual experiences. Teachers and curriculum writers assume that children in early childhood classrooms have little or no knowledge of geometric figures. Further, teachers have had few experiences with geometry in their own education or in their professional development. Thus, not surprisingly, most classrooms exhibit limited geometry instruction. One early study found that kindergarten children had a great deal of knowledge about shapes and matching shapes before instruction began. Their teachers tended to elicit and verify this prior knowledge but did not add content or develop new knowledge. That is, about two-thirds of the interactions had children repeat what they already knew. Therefore, teachers can be quite a bit more ambitious about the shapes they show and discuss.

A final type of relationship between shapes is equally important. Kindergartners should learn to describe the differences between two-dimensional ("flat") and three-dimensional shapes. Faces of three-dimensional shapes can be identified as specific two-dimensional shapes. Kindergartners also learn the names of more three-dimensional shapes, such as spheres, cylinders, prisms, and pyramids. They describe congruent faces of such shapes, such as the circle faces on opposite ends of a can. They begin to understand and discuss such properties as parallel faces in some contexts, such as building with blocks—where geometric and spatial structures are especially important. This brings us to the topic of spatial relations, in which geometric structure plays an even more important role.

Spatial Relations

Reasoning about spatial relations includes two main spatial abilities: spatial orientation and spatial visualization and imagery. Other important competencies include knowing how to represent spatial ideas and how and when to use such spatial knowledge in solving problems.

Spatial orientation involves knowing where you are and how to get around in the world. Similar to number, spatial orientation is a core cognitive domain—humans have competencies from birth. Children's skills are initially based on their own position and their movements through space, and soon increasingly include external references. Kindergartners should understand and use spatial terms, including *in, on, under, over, beside, next to, between, to the side of,* and *in front of.* They can begin to use the difficult relational terms *right* and *left* in both three-dimensional and two-dimensional contexts, using scaffolds and other guidance as needed (and they continue to develop left-right skills into the primary grades). The important consideration for educators is helping them *mathematize* these early competencies.

Spatial visualization involves building and manipulating objects mentally. Images are internal representations of objects that are structurally similar to their real-world counterparts. An image is not a "picture in the head." It is more abstract, more malleable, and less crisp than a picture. It is often segmented into parts. The spatial visualization considered here involves understanding and performing imagined movements of two- and three-dimensional geometric objects. Children need to be able to create a mental image and manipulate it.

Although many activities develop both these spatial abilities, we focus on each of them in turn. To develop *spatial orientation,* children might walk a path, remembering or drawing how they moved, and then try to make the

---

Using a Computer Program to Make Rectangles and to Recognize Squares as Special Rectangles

Kindergartner Chris is making shapes with a simplified version of the computer program Logo. He has been typing "R" (for "rectangle") and then two numbers for the side lengths. This time he chooses 9 and 9. He sees a square and laughs.

Adult: Now, what do the two 9s mean for the rectangle?

Chris: I don't know, now! Maybe I'll name this a *square rectangle!*

Chris uses his invented terminology repeatedly on succeeding days. His classmates started using it as well. This is a type of *logical structure*—one of "inclusion": All squares are also rectangles. It is helpful for teachers to use the term *square rectangle* because it can clarify the relationship between these two kinds of shapes: A square is a special rectangle that has all four sides equal (or as with Chris's shape, has any two adjacent sides of equal lengths).

turtle in the computer program Logo move along a similar path. The commands might be "FORWARD 100 RIGHT 90 [that is, turn to the right 90°] FD 40 LEFT 90 FD 50" (see fig. 3.5).

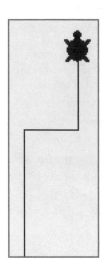

Fig. 3.5. A task to develop spatial orientation

Kindergartners might also build simple models of spatial relationships with such toys as houses, cars, and trees, as well as with blocks. Models and maps should eventually move beyond overly simple iconic picture maps and should challenge children to use geometric correspondences. Children must learn to deal with mapping processes of abstraction, generalization, and symbolization. Some map symbols are icons, such as an airplane for an airport, but others are more abstract, such as circles for cities. Children might first build with such objects as model buildings, then draw pictures of the objects' arrangements, then use maps that are "miniaturizations" and those that use abstract symbols. Teachers need to consistently help children connect the real-world objects to the representational meanings of map symbols.

Some children of any age will find it difficult to use a map that is not so aligned. It may help to give them experience with perspective. For example, they might identify block structures from various viewpoints, matching views of the same structure that are portrayed from different perspectives, or try to find the viewpoint from which a photograph was taken. Such experiences address such confusions of perspective as preschoolers' "seeing" windows and doors of buildings in vertical aerial photographs. Experiences with technological tools can help address these confusions. For example, teachers might use Google Maps or other similar Internet-based tools to "zoom in and out" so children see dynamically the relation of the school to the surrounding environment. Teachers might help children similarly view their own houses. Parents might be encouraged to help their children relate movements in a car to the maps and directions of GPS systems.

Equity in the education of spatial thinking is an important issue. Some studies indicate that early childhood teachers spend more time with boys than girls and usually interact with boys in the block, construction, sand-play, and climbing areas and with girls in the dramatic play area. Also, boys engage in spatial activities more than girls at home, both alone and with caregivers. Such differences may interact with biology to account for early spatial skill advantages for boys.

Fortunately, well-planned activities in kindergarten can provide all children with strong spatial competencies, and it is important for teachers to do so. For example, teachers should encourage girls to engage in these activities and interact with them as they do. Further, to *mathematize* such experience with boys or girls, teachers need to incorporate mathematical terms and concepts into these interactions. For example, teachers might ask girls to use blocks to build a bridge over the river they have made, or might remark on the symmetry in a house they have drawn and ask them to add windows that "keep the house symmetric." Such experiences close the spatial skills gaps that may separate girls and boys before school.

Kindergartners can learn to *structure space* as they attempt to cover a rectangular space with square tiles. Especially useful is attempting to *represent* their tilings with simple drawings. We return to this important skill in the measurement section because it is important to begin to develop understanding of area measure.

To develop spatial visualization abilities, kindergartners—like all young children—should have many experiences manipulating shapes, such as tangrams, pattern blocks, and other shape sets. Both "free exploration" activities, such as making buildings and pictures, and teacher-led activities are valuable. An example of the latter is a version of "Snapshots"—teachers secretly build a shape out of toothpicks, then show it to a small group of children for two seconds, then cover it again. Children try to build a copy.

Computers are especially helpful in developing spatial visualization abilities, as the screen tools make motions more accessible to reflection and thus bring them to an explicit level of awareness for children. For example, when children try to duplicate a picture they have made with physical shapes on the computer, they have to explicitly choose how to slide, turn, and flip computer versions of those shapes.

Many of the previously described shape activities also develop spatial visualization. One especially useful series of activities are the tactile-kinesthetic exploration of shapes. Also important is building and composing with two- and three-dimensional shapes, the core component to which we now turn.

Compositions and Decompositions in Space

The abilities involved in composing and decomposing shapes are important for many reasons. These geometric competencies are at the foundation of geometry, but also arithmetic (e.g., composing and decomposing numbers and arrays in multiplication), measurement, and higher-order geometric work, as well as such fields as architecture and the visual arts. Creating and then iterating units and higher-order units in the context of constructing patterns, measuring, and computing are established bases for mathematical understanding and analysis.

The early study of kindergartners described previously also found that too many of their teachers' attempts to add content were mathematically inaccurate. For example, one teacher said, "Every time you put two triangles together, you get a square." Not enough teachers possessed the knowledge to teach geometry well. Teachers have rarely had opportunities to explore and build sufficient geometric understanding themselves. So one important step to take is to switch from making assertions and generalizations to framing the same ideas as a question. "How many different ways can you put these two triangles together to make a new shape? What shapes will you get?" Then the children will see that even with two right triangles made from a square, they can put these together to make a triangle or a parallelogram (see

Making a Hexagon from Other Shapes

One child pulled her teacher over to show her a discovery. Putting three rhombi on top of the hexagon made the same shape. The teacher asked her to try to use other shapes to make a hexagon. The girl, and several of her friends, worked on the problem.

Child A: "I made it work with trapezoids. Two of them, one upsidedown from the other."

Child B: "It works with triangles!"

Child C: "How many did you need?"

Child B: "Ummm, one, two, three, four, five, six ... six!"

After a while, the teacher challenged them.

Teacher: "I have a hard question for you. Can you do it with squares?"

Five minutes of work convinced the class that it could not work.

The teacher had the girls show the class and challenge them to try it with squares. The children were excited. Ideas flew across the room.

"You just have to turn the squares the right way."

"No, they are never gonna fit."

Finally, one group stated confidently: "The angles are wrong! The square has square angles and the hexagon doesn't!"

The class agreed. The teacher concluded, "What an incredible moment of learning! I was elated!"

---

the bottom right of fig. 3.6). And teachers too will have time to consider all these relationships.

Given a supportive environment, including materials and interactions, young children show they also can do better thinking. The sidebar box "Making a Hexagon from Other Shapes" provides an example of children trying to compose a shape in different ways.

Kindergartners can develop the ability to intentionally and systematically combine shapes to make new shapes and complete puzzles. They do so with increasing anticipation, on the basis of the shapes' attributes, and thus, children develop mental imagery of the component shapes. That is, they move from using shapes separately (fig. 3.7) to putting them together to make pictures (fig. 3.8). A significant advance is that they can combine shapes with different properties, extending the pattern-block shapes (whose angles are multiples of 30 degrees) common at early levels to such shapes as tangrams (with angles that are multiples of 45 degrees), and with sets of various shapes that include angles that are multiples of 15 degrees, as well as sections of circles. Combining these shape sets should be done after children have worked with the pattern-block shapes separately from the square/rectangle/right triangle shapes based on 90 degrees and 45 degrees because many compositions are possible when the angles are consistent. Figure 3.6 shows the shapes in these various sets and how they depend on angles.

As a final illustration, computers can help children become aware of and mathematize their actions. For example, very young children can move puzzle pieces into place, but they do not think about their actions. Using the computer, however, helps children become aware of and describe these motions. Figure 3.9 illustrates one boy's picture, first constructed with physical pattern blocks. The computer also allowed him to recolor the shapes and add a background.

Using three-dimensional shapes, kindergartners can substitute a composite shape for a congruent whole shape. They learn to build complex structures, such as bridges, with multiple arches (e.g., fig. 3.10), with stairs at the ends. Providing such tasks to kindergarten children intentionally leads to great growth in spatial relations and can help close the gap between girls and boys in spatial skills. For example, an early problem might be to build an enclosure with walls that are at least two blocks high and include an arch. This construction introduces the problem of bridging, which involves balancing, measuring, and sometimes estimating. The second problem might be to build more complex bridges, such as bridges with multiple arches and ramps or stairs at the end. These constructions introduce planning and seriation. The third problem might be to build a complex tower with at least two floors, or stories. Children could be provided with cardboard ceilings, so that they have to make the walls fit the constraints of the cardboard's dimensions.

Kindergartners also can build structures with cubes or building blocks from two-dimensional pictures of these structures. Children of this age also can learn to move squares, rectangles, and right triangles on grids to create original designs. They also record these designs on squared-grid paper.

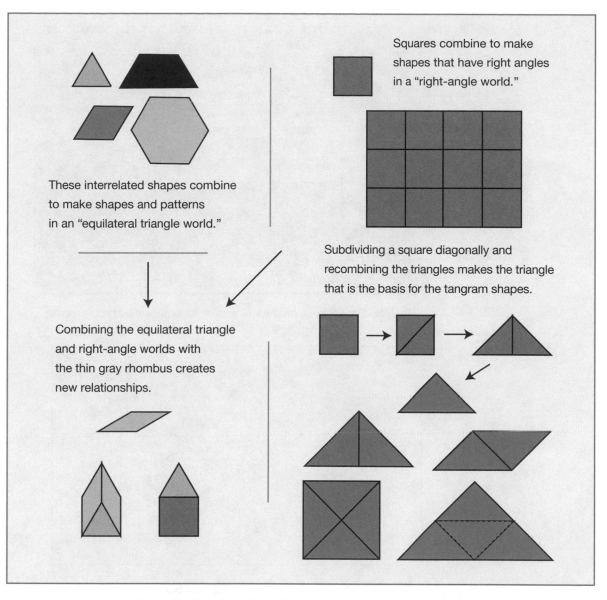

Fig. 3.6. Relationships within and among sets of shapes

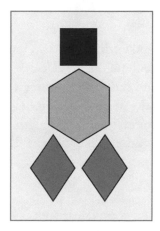

Fig. 3.7. Using shapes separately

Fig. 3.8. Composing shapes to make new shapes and pictures

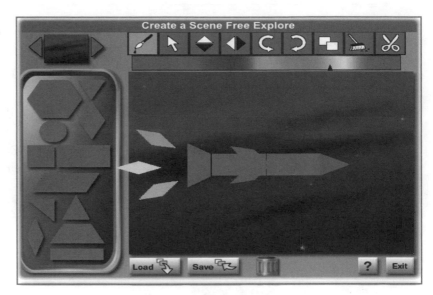

Fig. 3.9. Composing shapes to make new shapes and pictures

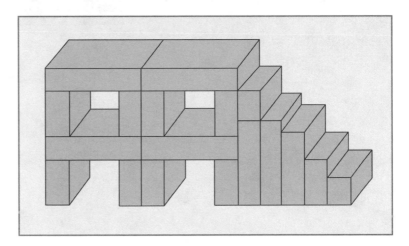

Fig 3.10. Building complex structures with bridges, arches, and stairs

Measurement

Geometric measurement[1] connects and enriches the two most important topics for early mathematics, geometry and number. Table 3.1 presents the developmental progressions for ideas and skills for measurement.

Measurement can be defined as the process of assigning a number to a magnitude of some attribute of an object, such as its length, area, or volume, relative to a unit, such as the length of the table in inches. These attributes are *continuous quantities*. In contrast, *discrete quantity* involves a number of sepa-

---

1. In this section, we describe children's development of *geometric* measurement—measurement in one, two, and three dimensions. We do not consider measurement of nongeometric attributes, such as weight/mass, capacity, time, and color, because these are more appropriately considered in science and social studies curricula.

rate things that can be determined exactly by counting with whole numbers, such as the number of people in a room. Measurement involves *continuous quantities*—amounts that can always be divided into smaller and smaller subunits such as centimeters, millimeters, micrometers (a millionth of a meter), and so forth.

Length

Length is a characteristic of an object found by quantifying how far it is between endpoints of the object. "Distance" is often used similarly to quantify how far it is between two points in space. Measuring length or distance consists of two aspects, identifying a unit of measure and *subdividing* the object by that unit: placing that unit repeatedly from one end to the other (*iterating* it) alongside the object (or placing multiple copies of that unit alongside).

From kindergarten through grade 2, children can significantly improve in measurement knowledge. Kindergartners can learn important measurement concepts, especially ordering objects by length and beginning to connect number to quantity, such as, "The length of my room is 10 feet and the area of its floor is 120 square feet." As stated previously, many U.S. students show limited understanding of measurement until after the primary grades. This limitation is not "developmental" but instead is a sign of limited, ineffective experiences with, and teaching of, measurement.

Kindergartners can learn to compare the length of two objects using a third object and transitive reasoning. For example, they can figure out that one path is longer than another because one path is longer than a piece of string but the other is shorter than that string.

Another important set of skills and understandings is ordering a set of objects. Such sequencing requires multiple comparisons. To complete the task efficiently also requires a systematic strategy, such as moving each new object "down the line" to see where it fits.

Such reasoning is important mathematically and is useful in many contexts, but it is not measurement until children assign a number to length. Kindergartners can learn to lay physical units, such as centimeter or inch manipulatives, end to end and count them to measure a length. They may initially iterate a unit leaving gaps between subsequent units or overlapping adjacent units. For such children, measuring may be a physical activity of placing units along a path in some manner rather than the activity of covering the space/length of the object with no gaps. As with transitive reasoning tasks, using comparison tasks, and comparing children's results with each others', can help reveal the limitations of such procedures and promote more accurate measuring. Children especially enjoy correcting a puppet that makes measuring mistakes that the teacher asks them to correct (see fig. 3.11).

To develop children's ability to quantify accurately in continuous and discrete situations, kindergartners should have a variety of experiences comparing the size of objects. Once they can compare lengths of objects by direct comparison, they should compare several items with a single item, such as finding all the objects in the classroom longer than their forearm. Ideas of

Math Talk about Counting and Units

A kindergarten teacher was never satisfied if her children just enumerated, as in "One, two, three, four." She would ask "How many?" If they answered "Four!" she was reassured they understood the cardinal—or "how manyness" principle.

However, she usually did not stop there. She would challenge children again: "How many *what*?" In measuring situations, children would yell, "Four meters!" or whatever the unit of measurement was. Even in discrete cases, the question can be relevant. She would ask her students the number of "whole people" in a set of Lego people, with three whole people and two "bottoms" and two "tops." Children would have to answer her question with a response such as "Five whole Lego people."

In measuring continuous quantities, and counting discrete quantities, it is important to remember the unit. This teacher's students did not measure a table with three-foot rulers and five-inch cubes and say it was "eight long"—they knew they had to have a consistent unit.

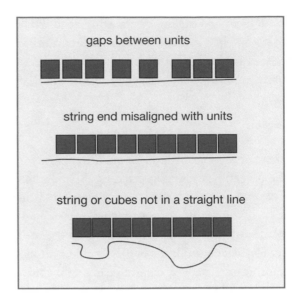

Fig 3.11. Measurement errors

transitivity can then be explicitly discussed as they use a string to represent their forearm's length.

Then children should engage in experiences that allow them to connect number to length. Provide children with manipulative units using standard units of length, such as centimeters or inches. Label these as "length-units" with the children. As they measure with these manipulatives, discuss the concepts and skills involved, such as not leaving space between successive length-units.

Discussions can focus on "What are you counting?" with the answer in "length-units" or "centimeters" or the like. Given that counting discrete items often correctly teaches children that the length-unit size does not matter, plan experiences and reflections on the use of units in various discrete counting and measurement contexts. See the sidebar box "Math Talk about Counting and Units." As another example, in a measurement context, the puppet that makes measuring mistakes might line up two large and two small blocks and claim a path is "four blocks long." Children can discuss whether he is correct. Comparing results of measuring the same object with manipulatives and with rulers helps children connect their experiences and ideas.

Area

The *area* of a shape is a measure of the amount of space inside the shape; it tells us how much material is needed to cover the shape (see fig. 3.12). Area measurement assumes that a suitable two-dimensional region is chosen as a unit, congruent regions have equal areas, regions do not overlap, and the area of the union of two regions that do not overlap is the sum of their areas. Finding the area of a region can be thought of as tiling a region with a two-dimensional unit of measure. To understand area effectively, children need to develop spatial structuring—the mental operation of organizing space into rows and columns. Such understandings are complex, and children develop them over time. These area understandings do not develop well in traditional U.S. instruction and have not for a long time, because children do not get experience in such spatial work.

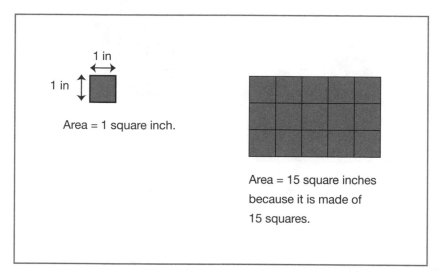

Fig. 3.12. The area of a rectangle

Children need to *structure an array*—a rectangular arrangement of squares—into rows and columns to understand area as truly two-dimensional. Learning spatial structuring is a long-term developmental process. Exploring with structured materials, such as unit blocks and square-inch tiles or blocks, can lay the groundwork for this understanding. With guidance, most kindergartners can learn to cover a rectangular space with physical tiles systematically. Some begin to represent their tilings with simple drawings.

In later grades, understanding area requires seeing how to decompose shapes into parts and how to move and recombine the parts to make simpler shapes whose areas are already known. Kindergartners might compare areas. For example, paper-folding activities lend themselves to equal-area, usually congruent, parts quite naturally. Some children can compare the area of two pieces of paper by cutting and overlaying them. They can learn to accurately count the number of squares in a rectangular array by using increasingly systematic strategies, including counting along rows or columns. Such experiences foster only initial development of area concepts, but these foundations are important for later learning.

Volume

The *volume* of a three-dimensional shape is a measure of the amount of material or space enclosed within the shape (see fig. 3.13). Volume introduces even more complexity than area. Adding a third dimension presents a significant challenge to students' spatial structuring—students need to think of rows, columns, and *layers* (height).

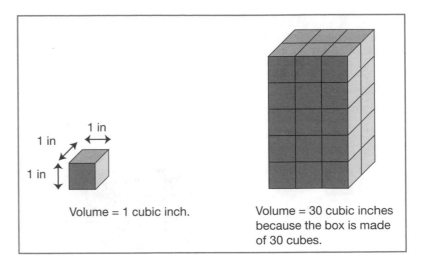

Fig 3.13. The volume of a box shape

Volume can also involve liquids or solids, thus leading to two ways to measure volume, illustrated by "packing" a space such as a three-dimensional array with cubic units and "filling" with iterations of a fluid unit that takes the shape of the container. For filling, the unit structure may be psychologically one-dimensional for some children. For example, children may simply "read off" the measure on a graduated cylinder.

Children can compare the volume of containers informally by pouring (water, sand, etc.) from one to the other (filling volume). They can make records that, for example, the container labeled "J" holds more than the container labeled "D" because when J is poured into D, it overflows. They may learn to use transitive reasoning, using a third container to compare the volumes of two others.

Kindergartners also can fill containers (into which cubes fit well) with cubes, filling one layer at a time intentionally (packing volume). They can also make buildings that have layers of rectangular arrays to see layers as they make them.

Geometry, Spatial Reasoning, and Measurement: Final Words

Geometric and spatial experiences are appropriate for, and achievable by, young children. They also contribute to their overall mathematical development. Such activities are also motivating to young children. Formal evaluations reveal that such activities contribute to children's development of both numerical and spatial/geometric concepts. Curricula that include substantial spatial and geometric activities show remarkably positive results. Children gain in geometric and spatial skills and show pronounced benefits in the areas of arithmetic and writing readiness in primary school. Children are better prepared for all school tasks when they gain the thinking tools and representational competence of geometric and spatial sense.

What if time is limited? What is most important? All the geometry and measurement content presented here is important and helpful for children and will prepare them for future learning. However, if your students enter kindergarten with little previous experience and you have only a half-day kindergarten, consider the following guidelines:

- Recognize that most spatial relations can be taught and practiced throughout the day, integrated into daily activities. However, they should be addressed intentionally and explicitly through targeted activities. Separate activities, such as making maps and models, are of secondary importance.

- Concentrate on the core knowledge and skills in shapes and structure, compositions and decompositions in space.

- Emphasize the spatial relations inherent in other geometry activities, such as those emphasized in the foregoing. For example, shape compositions can develop spatial visualization. "Close your eyes and picture a rectangle. Cut it from corner to corner. What would you get?"

- Measurement can be developed in other activities during the day. Initiate activity with comparing and ordering and decomposition experiences. Make sure that composition activities include making arrays of squares and cubes, which develops important spatial structuring skills and lays the groundwork for area and volume measurement.

4 Mathematizing: Solving Problems, Reasoning, and Communicating, Connecting, and Representing Ideas in Kindergarten

The general processes of problem solving, reasoning, and communicating, connecting, and representing ideas are important at every grade level and in all topics in mathematics. To make sense of mathematics and to connect mathematics to the world around them, students at all levels must actively think about mathematical ideas and seek to connect the ideas to their existing knowledge. To extend their knowledge, students at all levels must solve new problems, and they must discuss their solution strategies and ideas with others so that they can examine and refine those strategies and ideas. Teachers are important in these processes because they can set expectations about mathematics: that mathematics is a sense-making enterprise, that discussing and explaining our reasoning and ideas are important for learning, that mathematizing the world around us by examining everyday experiences from a mathematical point of view helps us understand both the world and mathematics better. Teachers can give children stimulating and enjoyable mathematical activities and problems in a nurturing math-talk environment that not only develops children's mathematical thinking but also satisfies children's curiosity, their eagerness to explore and learn, and their desire to engage with their peers and with adults.

In addition to these general processes of representing, reasoning, communicating, connecting, and problem solving, specific mathematical reasoning processes also exist that are important across all topics in mathematics, and that mathematics instruction should help children develop. These are—

- *unitizing*—finding or creating a unit, such as seeing 5 ones as a unit of five within 6 though 10 or recognizing that two right triangles with equal legs can make a square and using such squares to make patterns;

- *decomposing and composing,* such as decomposing a rectangle into two squares, or decomposing eight toy dinosaurs into a group of five and a group of three;

- *relating and ordering,* such as putting a collection of trucks in order by length or determining which collection of bears has more by matching; and

- *looking for patterns and structures and organizing information,* such as noticing that fingers have 5-groups and relating these to 5-groups shown with objects (such as eight toy dinosaurs) or sorting a collection of shapes according to whether they have three sides or four sides.

Examples of such processes have been given in this book for number and geometry. It is vital for parents and teachers to support children in using these mathematical processes.

Throughout this book we have provided snapshots of worthwhile activities for kindergarten children and some snippets of conversations to illustrate how you might engage children to extend their thinking and draw out mathematical ideas. We end with the suggestion that you revisit some of the examples given here, as well as some activities and environments that you already provide your students, and reconsider these activities with an eye toward engaging children in mathematical processes. Consider how you might further mathematize those activities and environments and enhance your classroom math talk to encourage reasoning, communicating, connecting, and representing mathematical ideas, and problem solving. Think about where you can help children unitize, decompose and compose, relate and order, and look for and describe patterns and structures and organize mathematical information. As you do so, consider seeking opportunities throughout the day for the following:

- Have children count objects, actions, and sounds and discuss with children that counting tells us how many there are.

- Encourage children to reason about how many objects are in a collection, especially when objects are grouped in certain ways (such as a group of five and one more).

- Ask children to compare collections and encourage reasoning about which has more or less.

- Provide opportunities for children to explore how to combine and take apart shapes or collections of things, and encourage children to discuss and reason about the process.

- Draw children's attention to features, attributes, and sizes of shapes and objects, including their edges, corners, and faces, and discuss how aspects of objects affect such things as whether they roll, stack, or fit in a space.

- Discuss relative locations of objects within the room or building or on the grounds to extend mathematical vocabulary.

Most of all, we encourage you to make learning the important mathematical ideas of early childhood active, engaging, and stimulating, for your students as well as for you.

References

Baroody, Arthur J.. and Ronald T. Coslick. *Fostering Children's Mathematical Power*. Mahwah, N.J.: Lawrence Erlbaum Associates, 1998.

Clements, Douglas H. "Subitizing: What Is It? Why Teach It?" *Teaching Children Mathematics* 5 (1999): 400–405.

Clements, Douglas H., and Julie Sarama. "Early Childhood Mathematics Learning." In *Second Handbook of Research on Mathematics Teaching and Learning,* edited by Frank K. Lester, Jr., pp. 461–555. New York: Information Age Publishing, 2007.

———. "Experimental Evaluation of a Research-Based Preschool Mathematics Curriculum." *American Educational Research Journal* 45 (2008): 443–94.

Cross, Christopher T., Taniesha A. Woods, and Heidi Schweingruber, eds. *Mathematics Learning in Early Childhood: Paths toward Excellence and Equity.* National Research Council, Center for Education, Division of Behavioral and Social Sciences and Education. Washington, D.C.: National Academy Press, 2009.

Fuson, Karen C. "Research on Learning and Teaching Addition and Subtraction of Whole Numbers." In *The Analysis of Arithmetic for Mathematics Teaching,* edited by Gaea Leinhardt, Ralph T. Putnam, and Rosemary A. Hattrup, pp. 53–187. Hillsdale, N.J.: Lawrence Erlbaum Associates, 1992a.

———. "Research on Whole Number Addition and Subtraction." In *Handbook of Research on Mathematics Teaching and Learning,* edited by Douglas Grouws, pp. 243–75. New York: Macmillan, 1992b.

———. *Math Expressions.* Boston: Houghton Mifflin Co., 2006, 2009.

Kamii, Constance K. *Young Children Reinvent Arithmetic: Implications of Piaget's Theory.* New York: Teachers College Press, 1985.

Kilpatrick, Jeremy, Jane Swafford, and Bradford Findell, eds. *Adding It Up: Helping Children Learn Mathematics.* National Research Council, Mathematics Learning Study Committee, Center for Education, Division of Behavioral and Social Sciences and Education. Washington, D.C.: National Academy Press, 2001.

National Council of Teachers of Mathematics (NCTM). *Curriculum Focal Points for Prekindergarten through Grade 8 Mathematics.* Reston, Va.: NCTM, 2006.

———. *Focus in Prekindergarten.* Reston, Va.: NCTM, 2009.

———. *Focus in Grade 1.* Reston, Va.: NCTM, forthcoming.

———. *Focus in Grade 2.* Reston, Va.: NCTM, forthcoming.

Piaget, Jean. *The Child's Conception of Number.* New York: W. W. Norton & Co., 1941/1965.

Ramani, Geetha B., and Robert S. Siegler. "Promoting Broad and Stable Improvements in Low Income Children's Numerical Knowledge through Playing Number Board Games." *Child Development* 79 (March–April 2008): 375–94.